COMPENDIUM OF THE CONFEDERATE ARMIES

LOUISIANA

COMPENDIUM OF THE CONFEDERATE ARMIES

LOUISIANA

Stewart Sifakis

AN INFOBASE HOLDINGS COMPANY

COMPENDIUM OF THE CONFEDERATE ARMIES: LOUISIANA

Facts On File, Inc.
460 Park Avenue South
New York NY 10016

Library of Congress Cataloging-in-Publication Data

Sifakis, Stewart.
Compendium of the Confederate armies.

Includes bibliographical references and indexes.
Contents: Alabama—Florida and Arkansas—Louisiana—North Carolina—Tennessee—Virginia.
ISBN 0-8160-2291-7
1. Confederate States of America. Army—History.
2. United States—History—Civil War, 1861–1865—Regimental histories. I. Title.
E546.S58 1992 973.7'42 90-23631

Text design by Ron Monteleone
Printed in the United States of America

MP FOF 10 9 8 7 6 5 4 3 2 1
This book is printed on acid-free paper.

To
the Memory of James Sifakis
1893–1961

CONTENTS

ACKNOWLEDGMENTS

I am deeply indebted for this work to the personnel, past and present, of Facts On File, especially to Edward Knappman, Gerry Helferich, and my editors: Kate Kelly, Helen Flynn, Eleanora von Dehsen, Traci Cothran, Nicholas Bakalar, Susan Schwartz and Michelle Fellner. Thanks also go to Joe Reilly, Michael Laraque, Jackie Massa and Kevin Rawlings. Also I would like to thank the staffs of the National Archives, Library of Congress, the various state archives and the New York Public Library for their patience and assistance. Over the past decades the staff of the National Park Service, Edwin C. Bearss, chief historian, have proven very informative on my frequent visits to the various battlefields. To Shaun and Christina Potter and Sally Gadsby I am indebted for keeping me at my work. For the logistical support of the management of the Hotel Post, Zermatt (Karl Ivarsson, Ursula Waeny and Lesley Dawkins), I am very grateful. And last, but certainly not least, I owe thanks to John Warren for his knowledge of computers, without which this project would have ground to a halt, and to his computer widow, Evelyne.

INTRODUCTION

This work is intended to be the companion set to Frederick H. Dyer's *Compendium of the War of the Rebellion* for the Confederacy. The compendium was first published as a three-volume work in 1909. A study of all the Union regiments, battalions, batteries and independent companies, it has since been reprinted in two- and one-volume editions.

It has been estimated that for every day since the end of the American Civil War, one book, magazine or newspaper article has appeared dealing with some aspect of that fratricidal struggle. Many ask: If so much has been written on the Civil War, is there really a need for more? The answer is an emphatic yes. Many aspects of the conflict have been covered only superficially and require much more in-depth research. But for such research a bedrock of reference works is essential.

There are many such works available, including the U.S. War Department's 128-volume *The War of the Rebellion: A Compilation of the Official Records of the Union and Confederate Armies* and the U.S. Navy Department's 31-volume *Official Records of the Union and Confederate Navies in the War of the Rebellion*. Registers of military personnel include: George W. Cullum's two-volume *Biographical Register of the Officers and Graduates of the United States Military Academy*, Francis B. Heitman's two-volume *Historical Register and Dictionary of the United States Army From Its Organization, September 29, 1789, to March 2, 1903*, Guy V. Henry's two-volume *Military Record of Civilian Appointments in the United States Army*, Robert K. Krick's *Lee's Colonels: A Biographical Register of the Field Officers of the Army of Northern Virginia* and Ezra J. Warner's *Generals in Gray: Lives of the Confederate Commanders* and *Generals in Blue: Lives of the Union Commanders*. Politics are covered in Jon L. Wakelyn's *Biographical Dictionary of the Confederacy* and Ezra J. Warner's and W. Buck Yearns' *Biographical Register of the Confederate Congress*. E. B. Long's *The Civil War Day by Day: An Almanac 1861-1865* provides an excellent chronology. Collective biographies include Mark M. Boatner's *The Civil War Dictionary*, Patricia L. Faust's

Historical Times Illustrated Encyclopedia of the Civil War and Stewart Sifakis' *Who Was Who in the Civil War*. Then, of course there is Dyer's compendium.

To date there has not been a comprehensive equivalent to Dyer's work for the South as a whole. Basically work has been done by individual states. North Carolina has an excellent work currently nearing completion. Other commendable works have been done for Tennessee, Virginia and Texas. Works were begun for Georgia and South Carolina but did not proceed far. State government agencies in Florida and Kentucky made some efforts in the early years after the war. However, none of these draws a consolidated picture of the Confederate States Army. That is where the *Compendium of the Confederate Armies* comes in.

This work is organized into volumes by state. One volume includes the border state units—Kentucky, Maryland and Missouri; units organized directly by the Confederate authorities from various state companies; and those units from the Indian nations allied with the Confederacy. The final volume consists of the tables of organization of the various armies and departments throughout the war.

There are chapters in each volume on the artillery, cavalry and infantry. Those units having a numerical designation are listed first, followed by those units using the name of their commander, home region or some other name. Units are then broken down alphabetically by size—for example, battalions, batteries, companies and regiments. If two or more units still have the same sorting features, they are then further broken down alphabetically by any special designation—1st or 2nd Organization, Local Defense Troops, Militia, Provisional Army, Regulars, Reserves, Sharpshooters, State Guard, State Line, State Troops or Volunteers and so on. The company designation for artillery batteries that served within an artillery battalion or regiment is listed at the end of the battalion or regiment designation. If heavy artillery battalions or regiments served together as a unit through most of the war, they are treated as a whole with no breakdown of the companies.

Each entry starts with the unit's name. Any nicknames or other mistaken designations follow. Then comes a summary of its organizational details: its date and location of organization, mustering into service, the number of companies for battalion organizations, armament for artillery batteries, surrenders, paroles, exchanges and disbandment or mustering out. The next paragraph starts with the first commanding officer and continues with an alphabetical listing of the other field-grade officers. (Captains are listed chronologically for artillery batteries.) The next paragraph is the brigade and higher-level command assignments of the unit. This is followed by a listing of the battles and campaigns the unit was engaged in. Note that the unit was not necessarily present on each date that is indicated for multiday actions. The final paragraph is the suggested further reading, if any.

Because records are incomplete, I have dropped the list of casualties of each unit that Dyer includes for the Northern units. But I have added to Dyer's format by including the first commanding officer and the field-grade officers of each unit. Selected bibliographies are included for each volume. Also, as available, unit histories and personal memoirs are listed with some units as suggested further reading.

LOUISIANA

LOUISIANA UNITS

Louisiana seceded from the Union on January 26, 1861.

There were several specialized types of units organized for the army. The Confederate Congress passed an act authorizing the creation of local Defense Troops units on August 21, 1861. However the Confederate Adjutant and Inspector General's Office did not issue its General Orders #86 outlining the regulations for their organization until June 23, 1863. These units were usually organized on the company and battalion level for defense of the areas in which they were raised. They were frequently composed of employees of government arsenals, armories, bureaus, etc. or from men detailed from regular line units for detached service. Toward the end of the war some of these units were organized into regiments. These units were only to be called into active service when the situation in the vicinity required it.

The Confederate Congress created the Reserves on February 17, 1864, when it expanded conscription to include all white males between 17 and 50. Those under 18 and those over 45 were to be organized in the Reserves, troops that did not have to serve beyond the boundaries of the state.

ARTILLERY

1. LOUISIANA 1ST FIELD ARTILLERY BATTERY

Nickname: St. Mary's Cannoneers

Organization: Organized and mustered into Confederate service at Franklin on October 7, 1861. Captured at Fort Jackson on April 26, 1862. Exchanged in mid-1862. It was designated as the 1st Field Artillery Battery on November 19, 1864. It was armed with two 24-lb. Howitzers and two 12-lb. Howitzers in May 1865. Surrendered by General E. K. Smith, commanding Trans-Mississippi Department, on May 26, 1865.

First Commander: Florian O. Cornay (Captain)

Captain: Minos T. Gordy

Assignments: Department #1 (October 1861-March 1862)

Fort Jackson, Forts Jackson & St. Philip [Higgins' Command], Coast Defenses [Duncan's Command], Department #1 (April 1862)

Artillery, District of West Louisiana, Trans-Mississippi Department (September 1862-December 1863)

Artillery, Mouton's-Polignac's Division, District of West Louisiana, Trans-Mississippi Department (December 1863-May 1864)

Faries' Artillery Battalion, Polignac's Division, District of West Louisiana, Trans-Mississippi Department (May-September 1864)

3rd (Faries') Mounted Artillery Battalion, 2nd (Polignac's) Division, 1st Corps, Trans-Mississippi Department (September-November 1864)

4th (Squires') Mounted Artillery Battalion, 1st (Forney's) Texas Division, 1st Corps, Trans-Mississippi Department (December 1864-March 1865)

3rd (Squiers') Field Artillery Battalion, 2nd (Polignac's-Thomas') Division, 1st Corps, Trans-Mississippi Department (March-May 1865)

Battles: New Orleans (April 18-25, 1862)

Fort Bisland [section] (April 13-14, 1863)

Irish Bend [two sections] (April 14, 1863)

Atchafalaya River *vs*. USS *Estrella* (June 4, 1863)

Atchafalaya River *vs*. gunboats (June 4, 1863)

vs. gunboats and transports on the Mississippi River (July 7-10, 1863)
Cox's Plantation, near Donaldsonville (July 12-13, 1863)
Hog Point *vs*. gunboats and transports (November 18-21, 1863)
Red River Campaign (May 10-22, 1864)
Mansfield (April 8, 1864)
Pleasant Hill (April 9, 1864)
Cane and Red Rivers Junction (April 26-27, 1864)
Mansura (May 16, 1864)
Yellow Bayou (May 18, 1864)

2. LOUISIANA 1ST ARTILLERY BATTERY REGULARS

See: CONFEDERATE 1ST ARTILLERY BATTERY REGULARS

3. LOUISIANA 1ST HEAVY ARTILLERY REGIMENT

Organization: Organized in militia service on February 5, 1861. Transferred to Confederate service on March 13, 1861. Companies B, C, D, E, F, H and K surrendered at the fall of Forts Jackson and St. Philip on April 26, 1862. These seven companies were exchanged in the fall of 1862. Regiment surrendered at Vicksburg, Warren County, Mississippi on July 4, 1863. Paroled at Vicksburg, Warren County, Mississippi in July 1863. Declared exchanged in early 1864. Six companies surrendered by Lieutenant General Richard Taylor, commanding the Department of Alabama, Mississippi, and East Louisiana, at Citronelle, Alabama on May 4, 1865.
First Commander: Paul O. Hébert (Colonel)
Field Officers: James B. Anderson (Major)
Daniel M. Beltzhoover (Major, Lieutenant Colonel)
William Capers (Major)
Henry A. Clinch (Major)
Johnson K. Duncan (Major)
Charles A. Fuller (Lieutenant Colonel, Colonel)
Raymond Montaigne (Major)
Assignments: Department #1 (March 1861-April 1862)
Forts Jackson and St. Philip [Higgins' Command], Coast Defenses [Duncan's Command], Department #1 [Companies B, C, D, E, F, H and K] (November 1861-April 1862)
Department #1 [Companies A, G and I] (May 1862)
Defenses of Vicksburg, Department #1 [Companies A, G and I] (May-June 1862)
Smith's Brigade, Department of Southern Mississippi and East Louisiana [Companies A, G and I] (June-July 1862)

Smith's Brigade, District of the Mississippi, Department #2 [Companies A, G and I] (July 1862)
2nd/3rd Sub-district, District of the Mississippi, Department #2 [Companies A, G and I] (July-October 1862)
Department of Mississippi and East Louisiana (October 1862)
2nd Military District, Department of Mississippi and East Louisiana (October 1862-January 1863)
Unattached, Smith's Division, 2nd Military District, Department of Mississippi and East Louisiana (January 1863)
Beltzhoover's-Lee's Brigade, Smith's Division, 2nd Military District, Department of Mississippi and East Louisiana (January 1863-April 1863)
River Batteries [Higgins' Command], Department of Mississippi and East Louisiana (April-July 1863)
Beltzhoover's Brigade, Forney's Division, Department of Mississippi and East Louisiana (November 1863-January 1864)
Fuller's-Higgins'-Fuller's Artillery Brigade, District of the Gulf, Department of Alabama, Mississippi, and East Louisiana (January 1864-January 1865)
Clinch's Artillery Battalion, Left Wing, Defenses of Mobile, Artillery Reserves, etc., District of the Gulf, Department of Alabama, Mississippi, and East Louisiana [Companies C & I] (March-April 1865)
Burnet's Command, Artillery Reserves, etc., District of the Gulf, Department of Alabama, Mississippi, and East Louisiana [Companies A, B, D, & G] (March-April 1865)
Fuller's Brigade, Department of Alabama, Mississippi, and East Louisiana [Companies C & I] (April-May 1865)
Burnet's Brigade, Department of Alabama, Mississippi, and East Louisiana [Companies A, B, D, & G] (April-May 1865)
Battles: New Orleans (April 18-25, 1862)
Vicksburg Bombardments [Companies A, G and I] (May 18-July 27, 1862)
Grand Gulf [Company A] (March 31, 1863)
Vicksburg Passage (April 16, 1863)
Grand Gulf [Company A] (April 29, 1863)
Vicksburg Campaign (May-July 1863)
Vicksburg Siege (May-July 1863)
Mobile Bay (August 5-23, 1864)
Mobile (March 17-April 12, 1865)

4. LOUISIANA 2ND HEAVY ARTILLERY BATTALION

Organization: Organized with six companies in northeastern Louisiana from October 1863 to February 1864. Surrendered by General E. K. Smith, commanding Trans-Mississippi Department, on May 26, 1865.

First Commander: George W. Logan (Lieutenant Colonel)
Field Officer: Eugene Soniat (Major)
Assignments: Unattached, District of West Louisiana, Trans-Mississippi Department (February-September 1864)
Siege Train, Trans-Mississippi Department (September 1864-May 1865)
Battles: Harrisonburg (March 1-4, 1864)
Red River Campaign (May 10-22, 1864)

5. LOUISIANA 2ND SIEGE ARTILLERY BATTERY

Also Known As: Battery B, Artillery Battalion, Miles' Louisiana Legion
Organization: Organized at Red River Landing ca. March 1, 1862. Surrendered at Port Hudson, Louisiana on July 8, 1863. Paroled in July 1863. Exchanged in the fall of 1863. Reorganized as a siege battery at Alexandria on December 12, 1863. Designated as the 2nd Siege Artillery Battery on November 19, 1864. Surrendered by General E. K. Smith, commanding Trans-Mississippi Department, on May 26, 1865. [NOTE: See also Louisiana Gibson's Artillery Battery; Louisiana Miles' Legion Infantry Battalion and Louisiana Miles' Legion Cavalry Battalion.]
First Commander: Richard M. Boone (Captain)
Captain: Samuel M. Thomas
Assignments: Department #1 (March-April 1862)
Port Hudson, Department #1 (April-June 1862)
Port Hudson, Department of Southern Mississippi and East Louisiana (June-July 1862)
1st Sub-district, District of the Mississippi, Department #2 (July-October 1862)
Department of Mississippi and East Louisiana (October 1862)
3rd Military District, Department of Mississippi and East Louisiana (October 1862-January 1863)
Maxey's Brigade, 3rd Military District, Department of Mississippi and East Louisiana (January 1863)
Buford's Brigade, 3rd Military District, Department of Mississippi and East Louisiana (March-April 1863)
Miles' Brigade, 3rd Military District, Department of Mississippi and East Louisiana (May-July 1863)
Artillery, Mouton's-Polignac's Division, District of West Louisiana, Trans-Mississippi Department (May 1864)
Faries' Artillery Battalion, Polignac's Division, District of West Louisiana, Trans-Mississippi Department (May-July 1864)
Siege Train, Trans-Mississippi Department (September 1864-May 1865)
Battles: Port Hudson *vs.* USS *Anglo-American* (August 29, 1862)
Port Hudson *vs.* USS *Anglo-American* and *Essex* (September 7, 1862)

Profit Island *vs*. USS *Winona* (December 13, 1862)

Natchez *vs*. USS *Indianola* [section aboard the CSS *Dr. Beatty*] (February 24, 1863)

Plains Store (May 21, 1863)

Red River Campaign (May 10-22, 1864)

Mansura (May 16, 1864)

Simsport (June 8, 1864)

Further Reading: Bergeron, Arthur, Jr. and Lawrence L. Hewitt, *Boone's Louisiana Battery: A History and Roster.*

6. LOUISIANA 3RD FIELD ARTILLERY BATTERY

Nickname: Bell Battery

Organization: Organized at Monroe in the spring of 1862. Designated as the 3rd Field Artillery Battery on November 19, 1864. It was serving as heavy artillery in May 1865. Surrendered by General E. K. Smith, commanding Trans-Mississippi Department, on May 26, 1865.

First Commander: Thomas O. Benton (Captain)

Assignments: Department #1 (May 1862)

District of West Louisiana, Trans-Mississippi Department (August-December 1862)

Sub-district of North Louisiana, District of West Louisiana, Trans-Mississippi Department (December 1862-January 1863)

Artillery, District of West Louisiana, Trans-Mississippi Department (January 1863-March 1864)

Artillery, Mouton's Polignac's Division, District of West Louisiana, Trans-Mississippi Department (March-May 1864)

Artillery, Green's-Bee's-Wharton's Cavalry Division, District of West Louisiana, Trans-Mississippi Department (May-June 1864)

Faries' Artillery Battalion, Polignac's Division, District of West Louisiana, Trans-Mississippi Department (August-September 1864)

3rd (Faries') Mounted Artillery Battalion, 2nd (Polignac's-Thomas') Division, 1st Corps, Trans-Mississippi Department (September 1864-May 1865)

Battles: Fort Beauregard (May 10-11, 1863)

Red River Campaign (May 10-22, 1864)

Mansfield [in reserve] (April 8, 1864)

Pleasant Hill [in reserve] (April 9, 1864)

Deloach's Bluff (April 26, 1864)

Chambers' Plantation (May 5, 1864)

Polk's Bridge, Bayou Lamourie (May 6, 1864)

7. LOUISIANA 4TH FIELD ARTILLERY BATTERY

Organization: Organized with recruits from Louisiana and Mississippi ca. August 1862. Designated as the 4th Field Artillery Battery on November 19, 1864. It was armed with one 12-lb. Howitzer and three 6-lb. Smoothbores in May 1865. Surrendered by General E. K. Smith, commanding Trans-Mississippi Department, on May 26, 1865.

First Commander: Archibald J. Cameron (Captain)

Assignments: Unattached, District of West Louisiana, Trans-Mississippi Department (August 1862-October 1863)

Harrison's Cavalry Brigade, District of West Louisiana, Trans-Mississippi Department (October-November 1863)

Artillery, District of West Louisiana, Trans-Mississippi Department (November 1863-September 1864)

4th (Squires') Mounted Artillery Battalion, 1st (Forney's) Texas Division, 1st Corps, Trans-Mississippi Department (September-November 1864)

Reserve Artillery Battalion, Trans-Mississippi Department (November 1864)

1st (Semmes') Horse Artillery Battalion, 2nd (Maxey's) Texas Cavalry Division, 1st Corps, Trans-Mississippi Department (December 1864-March 1865)

Unattached Artillery, Trans-Mississippi Department (March-May 1865)

Battles: Red River Campaign (May 10-22, 1864)

Ashton Landing, White River (July 24, 1864)

Sunnyside Landing (July 7, 1864)

8. LOUISIANA 5TH FIELD ARTILLERY BATTERY

Nickname: Pelican Artillery

Organization: Organized on October 31, 1862. It was armed with two 12-lb. Howitzers and two 3" Rifles in March 1864. Designated as the 5th Field Artillery Battery on November 19, 1864. It was armed with six 3" Rifles in May 1865. Surrendered by General E. K. Smith, commanding Trans-Mississippi Department, on May 26, 1865.

First Commander: Thomas A. Faries (Captain)

Captain: B. Felix Winchester

Assignments: District of West Louisiana, Trans-Mississippi Department (October 1862-April 1863)

Mouton's Brigade, District of West Louisiana, Trans-Mississippi Department (April-July 1863)

Major's Brigade, Green's Cavalry Division, Sub-district of Southwestern Louisiana, District of West Louisiana, Trans-Mississippi Department (September 1863)

Major's Brigade, Green's Cavalry Division, District of West Louisiana, Trans-Mississippi Department (September-October 1863)
Mouton's Brigade, District of West Louisiana, Trans-Mississippi Department (October-November 1863)
Mouton's Brigade, Mouton's Division, District of West Louisiana, Trans-Mississippi Department (November 1863)
Artillery, Polignac's Division, District of West Louisiana, Trans-Mississippi Department (November 1863-May 1864)
Faries' Artillery Battalion, Polignac's Division, District of West Louisiana, Trans-Mississippi Department (May-September 1864)
3rd (Faries') Mounted Artillery Battalion, 2nd (Polignac's) Division, 1st Corps, Trans-Mississippi Department (September-November 1864)
4th (Squiers') Mounted Artillery Battalion, 1st (Forney's) Texas Division, 1st Corps, Trans-Mississippi Department (December 1864-January 1865)
3rd (Squiers') Mounted Artillery Battalion, 2nd (Polignac's-Thomas') Division, 1st Corps, Trans-Mississippi Department (March-May 1865)
Battles: Petite Anse Island (November 21-22, 1862)
Bayou Teche [section] (January 14, 1863)
Fort Bisland (April 12-13, 1863)
Vermillion Bayou [section] (April 17, 1863)
vs. gunboats and transports on the Mississippi River (July 7-10, 1863)
Cox's Plantation, near Donaldsonville (July 12-13, 1863)
Stirling's Plantation [in reserve] (September 29, 1863)
Bayou Teche, near Patterson (November 3, 1863)
Hog Point *vs.* gunboats and transports (November 18-21, 1863)
Trinity [section] (March 1, 1864)
Harrisonburg [section] (March 1-4, 1864)
Red River Campaign (May 10-22, 1864)
Mansfield [in reserve] (April 8, 1864)
Pleasant Hill [in reserve] (April 9, 1864)
David's Plantation, Red River (May 12, 1864)
Marksville (May 15, 1864)
Mansura (May 16, 1864)
Moreauville (May 17, 1864)
Yellow Bayou (May 18, 1864)
Simsport (June 8, 1864)

9. LOUISIANA 6TH FIELD ARTILLERY BATTERY

Nickname: Grosse Tête Flying Artillery
Organization: Organized from paroled and exchanged men from the Pointe Coupie Artillery Battalion and transfers from the 1st Confederate Artillery

Battery Regulars ca. December 1863. Designated as the 6th Field Artillery Battery on November 19, 1864. It was armed with two 12-lb. Howitzers and two 2.90" Rifles in May 1865. Surrendered by General E. K. Smith, commanding Trans-Mississippi Department, on May 26, 1865.

First Commander: John A. A. West (Captain)

Captain: John Yoist

Assignments: Artillery, District of West Louisiana, Trans-Mississippi Department (November 1863)

Semmes' Horse Artillery Battalion, Green's Cavalry Division, District of West Louisiana, Trans-Mississippi Department (November 1863-September 1864)

1st (Semmes') Horse Artillery Battalion, 2nd (Maxey's) Texas Cavalry Division, 1st Corps, Trans-Mississippi Department (September 1864-March 1865)

1st (Semmes') Horse Artillery Battalion, 1st Corps, Trans-Mississippi Department (March-May 1865)

Battles: Red River Campaign (May 10-22, 1864)

Mansfield (April 8, 1864)

Pleasant Hill (April 9, 1864)

Blair's Landing (April 12, 1864)

Wilson's Landing, Red River (May 2, 1864)

Mansura (May 16, 1864)

Yellow Bayou (May 18, 1864)

10. LOUISIANA 8TH HEAVY ARTILLERY BATTALION

Nickname: Pinkney Battalion

Organization: Organized by the reduction and redesignation of the 8th Infantry Battalion with three companies on May 5, 1862. Battalion surrendered at Vicksburg, Warren County, Mississippi on July 4, 1863. Paroled at Vicksburg, Warren County, Mississippi in July 1863. Never reorganized following its exchange in early 1864. Some of the men went to Mobile and served with the 1st Heavy Artillery Battalion. The majority crossed the Mississippi River and reorganized as the 8th Heavy Artillery Battery in 1864.

First Commander: William E. Pinkney (Major, Lieutenant Colonel)

Field Officer: Frederick N. Ogden (Major)

Assignments: Department #1 (March-May 1862)

Defenses of Vicksburg, Department #1 (May-June 1862)

Smith's Brigade, Department of Southern Mississippi and East Louisiana (June-July 1862)

2nd/3rd Sub-district, District of the Mississippi, Department #2 (July-October 1862)

Department of Mississippi and East Louisiana (October 1862)
Unattached, 2nd Military District, Department of Mississippi and East Louisiana (October-December 1862)
Unattached, Smith's Division, 2nd Military District, Department of Mississippi and East Louisiana (December 1862-January 1863)
Beltzhoover's Brigade, Smith's Division, 2nd Military District, Department of Mississippi and East Louisiana (January-February 1863)
Lee's Brigade, Smith's Division, 2nd Military District, Department of Mississippi and East Louisiana (April 1863)
River Batteries [Higgins' Command], Department of Mississippi and East Louisiana (April-July 1863)
Battles: New Orleans (April 18-25, 1862)
Vicksburg Bombardments (May 18-July 27, 1862)
Vicksburg Passage (April 16, 1863)
Vicksburg Campaign (May-July 1863)
Vicksburg Siege (May-July 1863)

11. LOUISIANA 8TH HEAVY ARTILLERY BATTERY

Organization: Organized by the assignment of those exchanged members of the 8th Heavy Artillery Battalion west of the Mississippi River in 1864. Designated as the 8th Heavy Artillery Battery on November 19, 1864. Surrendered by General E. K. Smith, commanding Trans-Mississippi Department, on May 26, 1865.
First Commander: T. N. McCrory (Captain)
Assignment: Siege Train, Trans-Mississippi Department (September 1864-May 1865)

12. LOUISIANA 12TH HEAVY ARTILLERY BATTALION

Organization: Organized with two Louisiana, two Virginia, and one Alabama companies at Yorktown, Virginia in May 1862. Surrendered at Port Hudson, Louisiana on July 8, 1863. Paroled in July 1863. Exchanged in late 1863 or early 1864. Surrendered by Lieutenant General Richard Taylor, commanding the Department of Alabama, Mississippi, and East Louisiana, at Citronelle, Alabama on May 4, 1865.
First Commander: Paul Francis De Gournay (Major, Lieutenant Colonel)
Field Officers: George W. Logan (Major, Lieutenant Colonel)
Anderson Merchant (Major)

13. LOUISIANA 12TH HEAVY ARTILLERY BATTALION, COMPANY A

Nickname: Orleans Independent Artillery

Organization: Organized by the assignment of Company E, 1st Infantry Battalion, Zouaves in early 1862. Surrendered at Port Hudson, Louisiana on July 8, 1863. Paroled in July 1863. Some of the remnants served with the 1st Heavy Artillery Regiment. Others served independently around Mobile. Surrendered by Lieutenant General Richard Taylor, commanding the Department of Alabama, Mississippi, and East Louisiana, at Citronelle, Alabama on May 4, 1865.

First Commander: Paul Francis De Gournay (Captain)

Captain: John M. Kean

Assignments: Rains' Division, Department of the Peninsula (January-April 1862)

Rains' Brigade, D. H. Hill's Division, Department of Northern Virginia (April-May 1862)

Reserve Artillery, Army of Northern Virginia (May-August 1862)

1st Sub-district, District of the Mississippi, Department #2 (September-October 1862)

Department of Mississippi and East Louisiana (October 1862)

Heavy Artillery, 3rd Military District, Department of Mississippi and East Louisiana (October 1862-July 1863)

Higgins' Heavy Artillery Brigade, Department of the Gulf (January-April 1864)

Higgins'-Fuller's Heavy Artillery Brigade, District of the Gulf, Department of Alabama, Mississippi, and East Louisiana (April 1864-January 1865)

Clinch's Artillery Battalion, Left Wing, Defenses of Mobile, Artillery Reserves, etc., District of the Gulf, Department of Alabama, Mississippi, and East Louisiana (March-April 1865)

Clinch's Battalion, Fuller's Artillery Brigade, Department of Alabama, Mississippi, and East Louisiana (April-May 1865)

Battles: Yorktown Siege (April-May 1862)

Seven Days Battles [in reserve] (June 25-July 1, 1862)

Port Hudson *vs.* USS *Essex* (September 7, 1862)

Port Hudson Bombardment (March 14, 1863)

Port Hudson Siege (May-July 1863)

Mobile Bay (August 5-23, 1864)

Mobile (March 17-April 12, 1865)

14. LOUISIANA 12TH HEAVY ARTILLERY BATTALION, COMPANY B

Organization: Organized in May 1862. Surrendered at Port Hudson, Louisiana on July 8, 1863. Paroled in July 1863. Surrendered by Lieutenant General Richard Taylor, commanding the Department of Alabama, Mississippi, and East Louisiana, at Citronelle, Alabama on May 4, 1865.

First Commander: Felix Le Bisque (Captain)
Captain: Henry Castellanos
Assignments: Rains' Brigade, D. H. Hill's Division, Department of Northern Virginia (May 1862)
Reserve Artillery, Army of Northern Virginia (May-August 1862)
1st Sub-district, District of the Mississippi, Department #2 (September-October 1862)
Department of Mississippi and East Louisiana (October 1862)
Heavy Artillery, 3rd Military District, Department of Mississippi and East Louisiana (October 1862-July 1863)
Higgins' Heavy Artillery Brigade, Department of the Gulf (January-April 1864)
Higgins'-Fuller's Heavy Artillery Brigade, District of the Gulf, Department of Alabama, Mississippi, and East Louisiana (April 1864-January 1865)
Clinch's Artillery Battalion, Left Wing, Defenses of Mobile, Artillery Reserves, etc., District of the Gulf, Department of Alabama, Mississippi, and East Louisiana (March-April 1865)
Clinch's Battalion, Fuller's Artillery Brigade, Department of Alabama, Mississippi, and East Louisiana (April-May 1865)
Battles: Yorktown Siege (April-May 1862)
Seven Days Battles [in reserve] (June 25-July 1, 1862)
Port Hudson *vs.* USS *Essex* (September 7, 1862)
Port Hudson Bombardment (March 14, 1863)
Port Hudson Siege (May-July 1863)
Mobile Bay (August 5-23, 1864)
Mobile (March 17-April 12, 1865)

15. LOUISIANA 12TH HEAVY ARTILLERY BATTALION, COMPANY C

See: VIRGINIA HALIFAX ARTILLERY BATTERY

16. LOUISIANA 12TH HEAVY ARTILLERY BATTALION, COMPANY D

Nickname: Bethel [Virginia] Artillery
Organization: Organized in March 1862. A Virginia unit, it was assigned to this battalion in May 1862. Surrendered at Port Hudson, Louisiana on July 8, 1863. Paroled in July 1863. Surrendered by Lieutenant General Richard Taylor, commanding the Department of Alabama, Mississippi, and East Louisiana, at Citronelle, Alabama on May 4, 1865.
First Commander: W. Norris Coffin (Captain)
Assignments: Rains' Brigade, D. H. Hill's Division, Department of Northern Virginia (May 1862)

Reserve Artillery, Army of Northern Virginia (May-August 1862)
1st Sub-district, District of the Mississippi, Department #2 (September-October 1862)
Department of Mississippi and East Louisiana (October 1862)
Heavy Artillery, 3rd Military District, Department of Mississippi and East Louisiana (October 1862-July 1863)
Higgins' Heavy Artillery Brigade, Department of the Gulf (January-April 1864)
Higgins'-Fuller's Heavy Artillery Brigade, District of the Gulf, Department of Alabama, Mississippi, and East Louisiana (April 1864-January 1865)
Clinch's Artillery Battalion, Left Wing, Defenses of Mobile, Artillery Reserves, etc., District of the Gulf, Department of Alabama, Mississippi, and East Louisiana (March-April 1865)
Clinch's Battalion, Fuller's Artillery Brigade, Department of Alabama, Mississippi, and East Louisiana (April-May 1865)
Battles: Yorktown Siege (April-May 1862)
Seven Days Battles [in reserve] (June 25-July 1, 1862)
Port Hudson *vs.* USS *Essex* (September 7, 1862)
Port Hudson Bombardment (March 14, 1863)
Port Hudson Siege (May-July 1863)
Mobile Bay (August 5-23, 1864)
Mobile (March 17-April 12, 1865)

17. LOUISIANA 12TH HEAVY ARTILLERY BATTALION, COMPANY E

Nickname: Mohawk [Alabama] Artillery
Organization: Organized in May 1862. An Alabama unit. Surrendered at Port Hudson, Louisiana on July 8, 1863. Paroled in July 1863. Surrendered by Lieutenant General Richard Taylor, commanding the Department of Alabama, Mississippi, and East Louisiana, at Citronelle, Alabama on May 4, 1865.
First Commander: W. E. Seawell (Captain)
Assignments: Rains' Brigade, D. H. Hill's Division, Department of Northern Virginia (April-May 1862)
Reserve Artillery, Army of Northern Virginia (May-August 1862)
1st Sub-district, District of the Mississippi, Department #2 (September-October 1862)
Department of Mississippi and East Louisiana (October 1862)
Heavy Artillery, 3rd Military District, Department of Mississippi and East Louisiana (October 1862-July 1863)
Higgins' Heavy Artillery Brigade, Department of the Gulf (January-April 1864)
Higgins'-Fuller's Heavy Artillery Brigade, District of the Gulf, Department of Alabama, Mississippi, and East Louisiana (April 1864-January 1865)

Clinch's Artillery Battalion, Left Wing, Defenses of Mobile, Artillery Reserves, etc., District of the Gulf, Department of Alabama, Mississippi, and East Louisiana (March-April 1865)
Clinch's Battalion, Fuller's Artillery Brigade, Department of Alabama, Mississippi, and East Louisiana (April-May 1865)
Battles: Yorktown Siege (April-May 1862)
Seven Days Battles [in reserve] (June 25-July 1, 1862)
Port Hudson *vs.* USS *Essex* (September 7, 1862)
Port Hudson Bombardment (March 14, 1863)
Port Hudson Siege (May-July 1863)
Mobile Bay (August 5-23, 1864)
Mobile (March 17-April 12, 1865)

18. LOUISIANA 22ND HEAVY ARTILLERY REGIMENT

See: LOUISIANA 22ND (THEARD'S-HERRICK'S) INFANTRY REGIMENT AND LOUISIANA 22ND CONSOLIDATED INFANTRY REGIMENT

19. LOUISIANA BARLOW'S ARTILLERY BATTERY

Organization: Organized by detachments of cavalry at Montgomery, Alabama in the spring of 1864. It was armed with two 3.67" Sawyers and two 9-lb. Napoleons on May 19, 1864. Guns turned over to Battery F, 1st Mississippi Light Artillery Regiment in October 1864. The details returned to their original commands.
First Commander: William P. Barlow (Captain)
Assignments: District of Southwest Mississippi & East Louisiana, Department of Alabama, Mississippi, and East Louisiana (May-June 1864)
Scott's Brigade, W. Adams' Cavalry Division, Department of Alabama, Mississippi, and East Louisiana (June-August 1864)
Artillery, District South of Homochitto, Department of Alabama, Mississippi, and East Louisiana (August-October 1864)

20. LOUISIANA BELL ARTILLERY BATTERY

See: LOUISIANA 3RD FIELD ARTILLERY BATTERY

21. LOUISIANA BELTZHOOVER'S ARTILLERY BATTERY

See: LOUISIANA WATSON ARTILLERY BATTERY

22. LOUISIANA BENTON'S ARTILLERY BATTERY

See: LOUISIANA 3RD FIELD ARTILLERY BATTERY

23. LOUISIANA BOONE'S ARTILLERY BATTERY

See: LOUISIANA 2ND SIEGE ARTILLERY BATTERY

24. LOUISIANA BOUANCHAUD'S ARTILLERY BATTERY

See: LOUISIANA POINTE COUPÉE ARTILLERY BATTALION, COMPANY A

25. LOUISIANA BRIDGES' ARTILLERY BATTERY

Also Known As: South Carolina 18th Heavy Artillery Battalion, Company D

Organization: Organized by the assignment of those Louisianians serving in the 18th South Carolina Heavy Artillery Battalion at Charleston, South Carolina on February 13, 1864. Served as heavy artillery. Re-equipped as a light battery in March 1865. Surrendered by General Joseph E. Johnston at Durham Station, Orange County, North Carolina on April 26, 1865.

First Commander: William M. Bridges (Captain)

Assignments: 2nd Military District of South Carolina, Department of South Carolina, Georgia, and Florida (February-May 1864)

Taliaferro's Brigade, Department of South Carolina, Georgia, and Florida (July-December 1864)

Anderson's-Elliott's Brigade, Taliaferro's Division, Department of South Carolina, Georgia, and Florida (December 1864-February 1865)

Elliott's Brigade, Taliaferro's Division, Hardee's Corps (February-March 1865)

Manly's Artillery Battalion, 1st Corps, Army of Tennessee (April 1865)

Battles: Chapman's Fort, Ashepoo River (May 26, 1864)

Carolinas Campaign (February-April 1865)

Further Reading: Ripley, Warren, *Siege Train: The Journal of a Confederate Artilleryman in the Defense of Charleston.*

26. LOUISIANA BROWN'S ARTILLERY BATTERY

See: LOUISIANA GIBSON'S-BROWN'S ARTILLERY BATTERY

27. LOUISIANA BULL ARTILLERY BATTERY

See: LOUISIANA ST. MARTIN'S SIEGE ARTILLERY BATTERY

28. LOUISIANA BURSLEY'S ARTILLERY BATTERY

See: LOUISIANA WATSON ARTILLERY BATTERY

29. LOUISIANA CAMERON'S ARTILLERY BATTERY

See: LOUISIANA 4TH FIELD ARTILLERY BATTERY

30. LOUISIANA CHUST'S ARTILLERY BATTERY

See: LOUISIANA POINTE COUPÉE ARTILLERY BATTALION, COMPANY C

31. LOUISIANA CORNAY'S ARTILLERY BATTERY

See: LOUISIANA 1ST FIELD ARTILLERY BATTERY

32. LOUISIANA CRESCENT ARTILLERY BATTERY

Organization: Organized at New Orleans on March 27, 1862. It served as part of the crew of the CSS *Louisiana* in April 1862. Captured upon the fall of New Orleans on April 28, 1862. Reorganized at Jackson, Mississippi in December 1862. In 1863 it frequently served aboard the various vessels serving on the Red River. It was serving as heavy artillery from January 1864. Most of the company was captured at Fort De Russy, March 14, 1864. The remainder was surrendered by General E. K. Smith, commanding Trans-Mississippi Department, on May 26, 1865.

First Commander: T. H. Hutton (Captain)

Assignments: Department #1 [aboard the CSS *Louisiana*] (March-April 1862)

4th Military District, Department of Mississippi and East Louisiana (December 1862-January 1863)

Artillery, District of West Louisiana, Trans-Mississippi Department [frequently serving gunboat crews] (February 1863-September 1864)

Siege Train, Trans-Mississippi Department (September 1864-May 1865)

Battles: New Orleans [aboard the CSS *Louisiana*] (April 18-25, 1862)

Fort Taylor [capture of the USS *Queen of the West*] (February 14, 1863)

Capture of the USS *Indianola* on the Mississippi River [aboard the CSS *Webb*] (February 24, 1863)

Fort De Russy *vs.* USS *Albatross* [aboard the CSS *Grand Duke*] (May 4, 1863)

Red River Campaign (May 10-22, 1864)

Fort De Russy (March 14, 1864)

Simsport [detachment] (June 8, 1864)

33. LOUISIANA D'AQUIN'S ARTILLERY BATTERY

See: LOUISIANA GUARD ARTILLERY BATTERY

34. LOUISIANA DAVIDSON'S ARTILLERY BATTERY

See: LOUISIANA POINTE COUPÉE ARTILLERY BATTALION, COMPANY B

35. LOUISIANA DONALDSONVILLE ARTILLERY BATTERY

Organization: Organized and mustered in Confederate service in August 1861. It was armed with two 10-lb. Parrotts, one 3" Rifle, and three 6-lb. Smoothbores in August and September 1862. It was armed with one 10-lb. Parrott and two 3" Rifles on July 1-3, 1863. It was armed with two 12-lb. Napoleons and two 10-lb. Parrotts on December 28, 1864. Surrendered at Appomattox Court House, Virginia on April 9, 1865.

First Commander: Victor Maurin (Captain)

Captain: R. Prosper Landry

Assignments: Artillery, Department of the Peninsula (September 1861-January 1862)

Rains' Division, Department of the Peninsula (January-February 1862)

Unattached, Longstreet's Division, Department of Northern Virginia (April-June 1862)

Pryor's Brigade, Longstreet's Division, Army of Northern Virginia (June 1862)

Pryor's Brigade, Longstreet's Division, 1st Corps, Army of Northern Virginia (June-August 1862)

Pryor's Brigade, Wilcox's Division, 1st Corps, Army of Northern Virginia (August-September 1862)

Artillery Battalion, Anderson's Division, 1st Corps, Army of Northern Virginia (September 1862-May 1863)

Artillery Battalion, Heth's Division, 3rd Corps, Army of Northern Virginia (May-July 1863)

Garnett's-Richardson's Battalion, Artillery, 3rd Corps, Army of Northern Virginia (July 1863-April 1865)

Battles: Yorktown Siege (April-May 1862)

Williamsburg (May 5, 1862)

Seven Pines (May 31-June 1, 1862)

Seven Days Battles (June 25-July 1, 1862)

Gaines' Mill (June 27, 1862)

Frayser's Farm (June 30, 1862)

Beverly Ford and Rappahannock Station [skirmishes] [section] (August 23, 1862)

2nd Bull Run (August 28-30, 1862)

Antietam (September 17, 1862)

Shepherdstown Ford (September 19, 1862)

Fredericksburg (December 13, 1862)

Chancellorsville [not engaged] (May 1-4, 1863)

Gettysburg (July 1-3, 1863)

Williamsport [skirmish] (July 6, 1863)

Bristoe Campaign (October 1863)

Mine Run Campaign (November-December 1863)
The Wilderness (May 5-6, 1864)
Spotsylvania Court House (May 8-21, 1864)
North Anna (May 23-26, 1864)
Cold Harbor (June 1-3, 1864)
Petersburg Siege (June 1864-April 1865)
Petersburg Final Assault (April 2, 1865)
Fort Gregg (April 2, 1865)
Appomattox Court House (April 9, 1865)

36. LOUISIANA DURRIVE'S ARTILLERY BATTERY

Organization: Organized by its detachment from the 22nd (Theard's-Herrick's) Infantry Regiment in June 1863. Became Company B, 22nd Consolidated Infantry Regiment on January 26, 1864.
First Commander: Edward Durrive, Jr. (Captain)
Assignments: Ferguson's Brigade, Walker's Division, Department of the West (June 1863)
Reserve Artillery, Department of the West (July-June 1863)
Reserve Artillery, Department of Mississippi and East Louisiana (July-August 1863)
Cantey's Brigade, Department of the Gulf (September-October 1863)
Unattached, Department of the Gulf (November 1863)
Higgins' Brigade, Department of the Gulf (December 1863-January 1864)
Battle: Jackson Siege (July 10-17, 1863)

37. LOUISIANA ESHLEMAN'S ARTILLERY BATTERY

See: LOUISIANA WASHINGTON ARTILLERY BATTALION, 4TH COMPANY

38. LOUISIANA FARIES' ARTILLERY BATTERY

See: LOUISIANA 5TH FIELD ARTILLERY BATTERY

39. LOUISIANA FENNER'S ARTILLERY BATTERY

Organization: Organized at New Orleans on April 15, 1862. Mustered into Confederate service at Jackson, Mississippi on May 16, 1862. It was armed with two 6-lb. Smoothbores, two 6-lb. Rifles, and two 12-lb. Howitzers from October 24, 1862 to July 1863. It was armed with two 6-lb. Smoothbores and two 12-lb. Howitzers from December 12, 1863 to March 29, 1864. Surrendered by Lieutenant Richard Taylor, commanding the Department of Alabama, Mississippi, and East Louisiana, at Citronelle, Alabama on May 4, 1865. Actually surrendered at Meridian, Mississippi on May 10, 1865.
First Commander: Charles E. Fenner (Captain)

Assignments: Department #1 (April-June 1862)
Department of Southern Mississippi and East Louisiana (June-July 1862)
1st Sub-district, District of the Mississippi, Department #2 (July-October 1862)
Department of Mississippi and East Louisiana (October 1862)
3rd Military District, Department of Mississippi and East Louisiana (October 1862-January 1863)
Maxey's Brigade, 3rd Military District, Department of Mississippi and East Louisiana (January-May 1863)
Maxey's Brigade, Loring's Division, Department of the West (May-June 1863)
Maxey's Brigade, French's Division, Department of the West (June-July 1863)
Artillery Battalion, French's Division, Department of Mississippi and East Louisiana (July-August 1863)
Maxey's Brigade, French's Division, Department of Mississippi and East Louisiana (August-September 1863)
Cantey's Brigade, Department of the Gulf (September-November 1863)
Artillery Battalion, Stewart's Division, 2nd Corps, Army of Tennessee (December 1863-February 1864)
Eldridge's Battalion, Artillery, 2nd Corps, Army of Tennessee (February 1864-January 1865)
Hoxton's Artillery Battalion, Left Wing, Defenses of Mobile, Artillery Reserves, etc., District of the Gulf, Department of Alabama, Mississippi, and East Louisiana (March-April 1865)
Hoxton's Battalion, Fuller's Artillery Regiment, Department of Alabama, Mississippi, and East Louisiana (April-May 1865)
Battles: Jackson Siege (July 10-17, 1863)
Chattanooga Siege (September-November 1863)
Chattanooga (November 23-25, 1863)
Atlanta Campaign (May-September 1864)
Mill Creek Gap (May 8-11, 1864)
Rocky Face Ridge (May 9, 1864)
Resaca (May 14-15, 1864)
New Hope Church (May 25-June 4, 1864)
Atlanta Siege (July-September 1864)
Nashville (December 15-16, 1864)
Mobile (March 17-April 12, 1865)

40. LOUISIANA FULLER'S ARTILLERY BATTERY

See: LOUISIANA ST. MARTIN'S SIEGE ARTILLERY BATTERY

41. LOUISIANA GIBSON'S-BROWN'S ARTILLERY BATTERY

Also Known As: Company A, Artillery Battalion, Miles' Louisiana Legion

Organization: Organized at New Orleans in January 1862. Merged into Guibor's (Missouri) Artillery Battery on June 30, 1862. [NOTE: See also Louisiana Miles' Legion, Infantry Battalion; Louisiana Miles' Legion; Cavalry Battalion; and Louisiana 2nd Siege Artillery Battery
First Commander: Claude Gibson (Captain)
Captain: M. Brown
Assignments: Department #1 (January-February 1862)
District of North Alabama, Department of Alabama and West Florida (February 1862)
Pond's Brigade, 1st Corps, 2nd Grand Division, Army of the Mississippi, Department #2 (March 1862)
Reserve Artillery, Department #2 (March-June 1862)
Battles: Pittsburg Landing (March 1, 1862)
Corinth Campaign (April-June 1862)
Further Reading: Bergeron, Arthur, Jr. and Lawrence L. Hewitt, *Miles' Legion: A History and Roster.*

42. LOUISIANA GIRARDEY'S ARTILLERY BATTERY

See: LOUISIANA GUARD ARTILLERY BATTERY AND ALSO LOUISIANA ORLEANS GUARD ARTILLERY BATTERY, BATTERY A

43. LOUISIANA GORDY'S ARTILLERY BATTERY

See: LOUISIANA 1ST FIELD ARTILLERY BATTERY

44. LOUISIANA GREEN'S ARTILLERY BATTERY

See: LOUISIANA GUARD ARTILLERY BATTERY

45. LOUISIANA GROSSE TÊTE FLYING ARTILLERY BATTERY

See: LOUISIANA 6TH FIELD ARTILLERY BATTERY

46. LOUISIANA GUARD ARTILLERY BATTERY

Organization: Organized by the conversion of Company B, 1st Louisiana Infantry to artillery service on July 21, 1861. It was armed with two 3" Rifles and one 10-lb. Parrott in August and September 1862. It was armed with four 12-lb. Napoleons on December 28, 1864. Surrendered at Appomattox Court House, Virginia on April 9, 1865.
First Commander: Camille E. Girardey (Captain)
Captains: Louis E. D'Aquin
Charles Thompson
Charles A. Green
Assignments: Department of Norfolk (July 1861-January 1862)

Saunders' Artillery Battalion, Department of Norfolk (January-February 1862)
Blanchard's Brigade, Department of Norfolk (February-April 1862)
Artillery Battalion, Huger's-Anderson's Division, Army of Northern Virginia (April-July 1862)
Artillery Battalion, Anderson's Division, 1st Corps, Army of Northern Virginia (July-August 1862)
Artillery Battalion, Ewell's-Early's Division, 2nd Corps, Army of Northern Virginia (August 1862-April 1863)
Jones' Artillery Battalion, Jackson's-Trimble's-Colston's Division, 2nd Corps, Army of Northern Virginia (April-May 1863)
Jones' Artillery Battalion, Early's Division, 2nd Corps, Army of Northern Virginia (May-July 1863)
Jones' Battalion, Artillery, 2nd Corps, Army of Northern Virginia (July 1863-January 1864)
Unattached, Richmond Defenses, Department of Richmond (February-September 1864)
Stark's Artillery Battalion, Richmond Defenses, Department of Richmond (September-October 1864)
Stark's Battalion, Artillery, 1st Corps, Army of Northern Virginia (October 1864-February 1865)
Stark's Battalion, Artillery, 2nd Corps, Army of Northern Virginia (March-April 1865)
Battles: Cedar Mountain (August 9, 1862)
2nd Bull Run (August 28-30, 1862)
Harpers Ferry (September 12-15, 1862)
Antietam (September 17, 1862)
Fredericksburg (December 13, 1862)
Chancellorsville (May 1-4, 1863)
2nd Winchester (June 14-15, 1863)
Gettysburg (July 1-3, 1863)
Hunterstown (July 2, 1863)
Bristoe Campaign (October 1863)
Rappahannock Station (November 7, 1863)
Mine Run Campaign (November-December 1863)
Petersburg Siege (June 1864-April 1865)
Chaffin's Farm (September 29-30, 1864)
Fort Gilmer (September 29-30, 1864)
Appomattox Court House (April 9, 1865)

47. LOUISIANA HERO'S ARTILLERY BATTERY

See: LOUISIANA WASHINGTON ARTILLERY BATTALION, 3RD COMPANY

48. LOUISIANA HOLMES'-ROBINSON'S ARTILLERY BATTERY

Organization: Organized as the howitzer battery attached to the 1st Cavalry Regiment in September 1861. Disbanded in December 1863. Reorganized at Clinton, Louisiana on March 24, 1864. It was armed with two 6-lb. Smoothbores and two 12-lb. Howitzers on May 19, 1864. It was temporarily attached to Bradford's Battery F, 1st Mississippi Light Artillery Regiment. Surrendered by Lieutenant General Richard Taylor, commanding the Department of Alabama, Mississippi, and East Louisiana, at Citronelle, Alabama on May 4, 1865.

First Commander: William H. Holmes (Lieutenant)

Captain: Eugene H. Holmes

Field Officer: N. T. N. Robinson (Captain, Major)

Assignments: Scott's Cavalry Brigade, Department of East Tennessee (October-November 1862)

Pegram's Brigade, Wheeler's Cavalry Division, Army of Tennessee (November 1862-January 1863)

Pegram's Cavalry Brigade, Department of East Tennessee (January-April 1863)

Scott's Cavalry Brigade, Army of Tennessee (July-August 1863)

Scott's Brigade, Pegram's Division, Forrest's Cavalry Corps, Army of Tennessee (September-November 1863)

District of Southwest Mississippi and East Louisiana, Department of Alabama, Mississippi, and East Louisiana (March-June 1864)

Unattached, W. Adams' Cavalry Division, Department of Alabama, Mississippi, and East Louisiana (June-July 1864)

Scott's Brigade, W. Adams' Cavalry Division, Department of Alabama, Mississippi, and East Louisiana (July-August 1864)

Artillery, District South of Homochitto, Department of Alabama, Mississippi, and East Louisiana (August 1864-January 1865)

Burnet's Command, Artillery Reserves, etc., District of the Gulf, Department of Alabama, Mississippi, and East Louisiana (March-April 1865)

Burnet's Command, Department of Alabama, Mississippi, and East Louisiana (April-May 1865)

Battles: Athens (May 1-2, 1862)

Scott's Eastern Kentucky Raid (July 25-August 6, 1863)

Big Hill (August 23, 1862)

Chickamauga (September 19-20, 1863)

Chattanooga Siege (September-November 1863)

Chattanooga (November 23-25, 1863)

Woodville (October 5, 1864)

Mobile (March 17-April 12, 1865)

49. LOUISIANA HUTTON'S ARTILLERY BATTERY

See: LOUISIANA CRESCENT ARTILLERY BATTERY

50. LOUISIANA KING'S SIEGE ARTILLERY BATTERY

See: LOUISIANA ST. MARTIN'S SIEGE ARTILLERY BATTERY

51. LOUISIANA LANDRY'S ARTILLERY BATTERY

See: LOUISIANA DONALDSONVILLE ARTILLERY BATTERY

52. LOUISIANA LE GARDEUR'S ARTILLERY BATTERY

See: LOUISIANA ORLEANS ARTILLERY BATTERY, BATTERY A

53. LOUISIANA MCCRORY'S ARTILLERY BATTERY

See: LOUISIANA 8TH HEAVY ARTILLERY BATTERY

54. LOUISIANA MADISON ARTILLERY BATTERY

Nickname: Madison Tips

Organization: Organized as an infantry unit at New Carthage in the spring of 1861. Mustered into Confederate service at Lynchburg, Virginia on May 23, 1861. Converted to artillery service on August 23, 1862. It was armed with two 12-lb. Howitzers, two 3" Rifles, and two 6-lb. Smoothbores on June 26 to July 1, 1862. It was armed with two 3" Rifles and two 24-lb. Howitzers in August and September 1862. It was armed with four 24-lb. Howitzers on July 1-3, 1863. It was armed with four 24-lb. Howitzers and two 12-lb. Howitzers on December 28, 1864. Surrendered at Appomattox Court House, Virginia on April 9, 1865.

First Commander: George V. Moody (Captain)

Assignments: Hampton's Brigade, G. W. Smith's-Whiting's Division, Department of Northern Virginia (April-June 1862)

Garnett's Artillery Battalion, D. R. Jones' Division, Army of Northern Virginia (June-July 1862)

Toombs' Brigade, D. R. Jones' Division, 1st Corps, Army of Northern Virginia (July-August 1862)

Lee's-Alexander's Battalion, Artillery Reserve, 1st Corps, Army of Northern Virginia (August 1862-July 1863)

Alexander's Battalion, Artillery, 1st Corps, Army of Northern Virginia (July-September 1863)

Alexander's Battalion, Artillery, Longstreet's Corps, Army of Tennessee (September-November 1863)

Alexander's-Huger's Battalion, Artillery, Department of East Tennessee (November 1863-April 1864)

Huger's Battalion, Artillery, 1st Corps, Army of Northern Virginia (April 1864-April 1865)

Battles: Yorktown Siege (April-May 1862)
Seven Days Battles (June 25-July 1, 1862)
Garnett's Farm (June 28, 1862)
Golding's Farm (June 28, 1862)
Fair Oaks Station (June 29, 1862)
2nd Manassas Campaign [not engaged] (August 1862)
Antietam (September 17, 1862)
Fredericksburg (December 13, 1862)
Chancellorsville (May 1-4, 1863)
Gettysburg (July 1-3, 1863)
Chickamauga [not engaged] (September 19-20, 1863)
Chattanooga Siege (September-November 1863)
Knoxville Siege (November 1863)
The Wilderness (May 5-6, 1864)
Spotsylvania Court House (May 8-21, 1864)
North Anna (May 23-26, 1864)
Cold Harbor (June 1-3,1864)
Petersburg Siege (June 1864-April 1865)
Appomattox Court House (April 9, 1865)

55. LOUISIANA MAURIN'S ARTILLERY BATTERY

See: LOUISIANA DONALDSONVILLE ARTILLERY BATTERY

56. LOUISIANA MILES' LEGION ARTILLERY BATTALION, COMPANY A

See: LOUISIANA GIBSON'S-BROWN'S ARTILLERY BATTERY

57. LOUISIANA MILES' LEGION ARTILLERY BATTALION, COMPANY B

See: LOUISIANA 2ND SIEGE ARTILLERY BATTERY

58. LOUISIANA MILLER'S ARTILLERY BATTERY

See: LOUISIANA WASHINGTON ARTILLERY BATTALION, 3RD COMPANY

59. LOUISIANA MOODY'S ARTILLERY BATTERY

See: LOUISIANA MADISON ARTILLERY BATTERY

60. LOUISIANA NORCOM'S ARTILLERY BATTERY

See: LOUISIANA WASHINGTON ARTILLERY BATTALION, 4TH COMPANY

61. LOUISIANA ORLEANS GUARD, ARTILLERY BATTERY

Organization: Organized at New Orleans on March 6, 1862. Organized for ninety days in Confederate service in March 1862. It was armed with four 6-lb. Smoothbores and two 12-lb. Howitzers in March 1862. Battery merged into the 10th Missouri Artillery Battery on July 21, 1862. NOTE: This battery was part of the same corps as the Orleans Guard Infantry Battalion.

First Commander: Henry Ducatel (Captain)

Assignments: Department #1 (March 1862)

Mouton's-Gober's-Reichard's Brigade, Ruggles' Division, 2nd Corps, Army of the Mississippi, Department #2 (April-June 1862)

Reichard's Brigade, 2nd Corps, Army of the Mississippi, Department #2 (June-July 1862)

Reichard's Brigade, Jones' Division, Army of the Mississippi, Department #2 (July 1862)

Battles: Corinth Campaign (April-June 1862)

Farmington (May 9, 1862)

62. LOUISIANA ORLEANS GUARD ARTILLERY BATTERY, BATTERY A

Organization: Organized by detaching those members of the 10th Missouri Artillery Battery who had previously served in the Orleans Guard Artillery Battery and forming this new company on July 11, 1863, per S.O. #183, Army of Tennessee. This battery received the guns of the Chestatee (Georgia) Artillery Battery upon its arrival at Charleston, South Carolina in November 1863. It was armed with two 6-lb. Smoothbores and two 12-lb. Howitzers from April 2, 1864 to May 3, 1864. It was armed with four 12-lb. Napoleons and two 3.5" Blakelys on January 6, 1865.

First Commander: G. Le Gardeur, Jr. (Captain)

Captain: Camille E. Girardey

Assignments: Artillery Reserve, Army of Tennessee (July-September 1863)

Robertson's Battalion, Artillery Reserve, Army of Tennessee (September-November 1863)

Unattached, 1st Military District of South Carolina, Department of South Carolina, Georgia and Florida (November 1863-July 1864)

Ripley's Brigade, Department of South Carolina, Georgia, and Florida (July-August 1864)

Taliaferro's Brigade, Department of South Carolina, Georgia, and Florida (October-December 1864)

2nd Light Artillery Battery, Taliaferro's Division, Department of South Carolina, Georgia, and Florida (December 1864-January 1865)
Rhett's Brigade, Taliaferro's Division, Department of South Carolina, Georgia, and Florida (January-February 1865)
Rhett's Artillery Battalion, Taliaferro's Division, Hardee's Corps (February-March 1865)
Rhett's Battalion, Artillery, Hardee's Corps (March-April 1865)
Rhett's Artillery Battalion, 3rd Corps, Army of Tennessee (April 1865)
Battles: Chickamauga (September 19-20, 1863)
Chattanooga Siege (September-November 1863)
Fort Johnson and Battery Simkins (July 10, 1864)
Carolinas Campaign (February-April 1865)
Averasboro (March 16, 1865)

63. LOUISIANA OWENS' ARTILLERY BATTERY

See: LOUISIANA WASHINGTON ARTILLERY BATTALION, 1ST COMPANY

64. LOUISIANA PELICAN ARTILLERY BATTERY

See: LOUISIANA 5TH FIELD ARTILLERY BATTERY

65. LOUISIANA POINTE COUPÉE ARTILLERY BATTALION

Organization: Organized and mustered in as a single battery ca. August 1861. Increased to a battalion at Abbeville, Mississippi ca. August 1862. Many of the paroled and exchanged prisoners ended up in the 6th Field Artillery Battery ca. December 1863. SEE: Individual batteries following.
First Commander: R. A. Stewart (Major)

66. LOUISIANA POINTE COUPÉE ARTILLERY BATTALION, COMPANY A

Organization: Organized ca. August 1861. It was armed with one 10-lb. Parrott, two 12-lb. Howitzers, and three 6-lb. Smoothbores on April 6, 1862. One section surrendered at Vicksburg, Warren County, Mississippi on July 4, 1863. Paroled at Vicksburg, Warren County, Mississippi in July 1863. Many of the paroled and exchanged prisoners ended up in the 6th Field Artillery Battery ca. December 1863. That section of Company C not surrendered at Vicksburg was merged into this battery. It was armed with four 12-lb. Howitzers from November 28, 1863 to January 5, 1864. It was armed with four 12-lb. Napoleons on May 1, 1864. Virtually wiped out at Nashville, Tennessee on December 15-16, 1864. Remnants surrendered by Lieutenant General Richard Taylor, commanding the Department of Alabama, Mississippi, and East Louisiana, at Citronelle, Alabama on May 4, 1865.

First Commander: R. A. Stewart (Captain)

Captain: Alcide Bouanchaud

Assignments: McCown's Brigade, 1st Geographical Division, Department #2 (September-October 1861)

Neely's Brigade, McCown's Division, 1st Geographical Division, Department #2 (October 1861-February 1862)

Unattached, McCown's Command, 1st Geographical Division, Department #2 (February-March 1862)

Gantt's Brigade, McCown's Command, 1st Geographical Division, Department #2 (March-April 1862)

Fort Pillow, Department #2 (April-May 1862)

Grenada, Mississippi, Department #2 (June 1862)

Department of Mississippi and East Louisiana (October 1862)

Artillery, Tilghman's Division, Army of West Tennessee, Department of Mississippi and East Louisiana (December 1862)

Artillery, Tilghman's Division, Lovell's Corps, Army of North Mississippi, Department of Mississippi and East Louisiana (December 1862-January 1863)

Rust's Brigade, Loring's Division, Army of the Department of Mississippi and East Louisiana (January-February 1863)

Rust's Brigade, 3rd Military District, Department of Mississippi and East Louisiana (March-April 1863)

4th Military District, Department of Mississippi and East Louisiana (April-May 1863)

Buford's Brigade, Loring's Division, Department of Mississippi and East Louisiana (May 1863)

Barton's Brigade, Stevenson's Division, Department of Mississippi and East Louisiana [section] (May-July 1863)

Buford's Brigade, Loring's Division, Department of the West (May-July 1863)

Buford's Brigade, Loring's Division, Department of Mississippi and East Louisiana (July 1863-January 1864)

Buford's Brigade, Loring's Division, Department of Alabama, Mississippi, and East Louisiana (January-February 1864)

Artillery Battalion, Loring's Division, Department of Alabama, Mississippi, and East Louisiana (March-May 1864)

Myrick's Artillery Battalion, Loring's Division, Army of Mississippi (May-July 1864)

Myrick's Battalion, Artillery, Army of Mississippi (July 1864)

Myrick's Battalion, Artillery, 3rd Corps, Army of Tennessee (July 1864-January 1865)

District of Central Alabama, Department of Alabama, Mississippi, and East Louisiana (February-March 1865)
District of Alabama, Department of Alabama, Mississippi, and East Louisiana (March-May 1865)
Battles: Belmont (November 7, 1861)
Island #10 (April 6-7, 1862)
Coffeeville (December 5, 1862)
Yazoo Pass (February 16-19, 1863)
Port Hudson Bombardment (March 14, 1863)
Grierson's Raid (April 17-May 2, 1863)
Vicksburg Campaign (May-July 1863)
Champion Hill (May 16, 1863)
Vicksburg Siege [section] (May-July 1863)
Jackson Siege (July 10-17, 1863)
Meridian Campaign (February-March 1864)
Atlanta Campaign (May-September 1864)
Atlanta Siege (July-September 1864)
Allatoona (October 5, 1864)
Nashville (December 15-16, 1864)

67. LOUISIANA POINTE COUPÉE ARTILLERY BATTALION, COMPANY B

Organization: Organized in early 1862. Battery surrendered at Vicksburg, Warren County, Mississippi on July 4, 1863. Paroled at Vicksburg, Warren County, Mississippi in July 1863. The battery never reorganized. Many of the paroled and exchanged prisoners ended up in the 6th Field Artillery Battery ca. December 1863.
First Commander: William A. Davidson (Captain)
Assignments: Neely's Brigade, McCown's Division, 1st Geographical Division, Department #2 (October 1861-February 1862)
Unattached, McCown's Command, 1st Geographical Division, Department #2 (February-March 1862)
Gantt's Brigade, McCown's Command, 1st Geographical Division, Department #2 (March-April 1862)
Fort Pillow, Department #2 (April-May 1862)
Grenada, Mississippi, Department #2 (June 1862)
Department of Mississippi and East Louisiana (October 1862)
Moore's Brigade, Loring's Division, 2nd Military District, Department of Mississippi and East Louisiana (March-April 1863)
Moore's Brigade, Loring's Division, Department of Mississippi and East Louisiana (April-May 1863)

Moore's Brigade, Forney's Division, Department of Mississippi and East Louisiana (May-July 1863)
Battles: Island #10 (April 6-7, 1862)
Coffeeville (December 5, 1862)
Yazoo Pass (February 16-19, 1863)
Fort Pemberton (March 11, 1863)
Fort Pemberton (March 13, 1863)
Fort Pemberton (March 16, 1863)
Fort Pemberton (April 2, 1863)
Fort Pemberton (April 4, 1863)
Vicksburg Campaign (May-July 1863)
Vicksburg Siege (May-July 1863)

68. LOUISIANA POINTE COUPÉE ARTILLERY BATTALION, COMPANY C

Organization: Organized ca. August 1862. Battery, except for one section, surrendered at Vicksburg, Warren County, Mississippi on July 4, 1863. Paroled at Vicksburg, Warren County, Mississippi in July 1863. That portion not surrendered was assigned to Company A. The battery never reorganized. Many of the paroled and exchanged prisoners ended up in the 6th Field Artillery Battery ca. December 1863.
First Commander: Alexander Chust (Captain)
Assignments: Department of Mississippi and East Louisiana (October 1862)
Rust's Brigade, 3rd Military District, Department of Mississippi and East Louisiana (March-April 1863)
4th Military District, Department of Mississippi and East Louisiana (April-May 1863)
Barton's Brigade, Stevenson's Division, Department of Mississippi and East Louisiana (May-July 1863)
Buford's Brigade, Loring's Division, Department of Mississippi and East Louisiana [section] (May 1863)
Buford's Brigade, Loring's Division, Department of the West [section] (May-July 1863)
Battles: Coffeeville (December 5, 1862)
Port Hudson Bombardment (March 14, 1863)
Vicksburg Campaign (May-July 1863)
Champion Hill (May 16, 1863)
Vicksburg Siege (May-July 1863)

69. LOUISIANA RICHARDSON'S ARTILLERY BATTERY

See: LOUISIANA WASHINGTON ARTILLERY BATTALION, 2ND COMPANY

70. LOUISIANA ROBINSON'S ARTILLERY BATTERY

See: LOUISIANA HOLMES'-ROBINSON'S ARTILLERY BATTERY

71. LOUISIANA ROSSER'S ARTILLERY BATTERY

See: LOUISIANA WASHINGTON ARTILLERY BATTALION, 2ND COMPANY

72. LOUISIANA ST. MARTIN'S SIEGE ARTILLERY BATTERY

Nickname: Bull Battery

Organization: Organized as a cavalry company on May 14, 1862. Converted to artillery service at Grand Encore, Louisiana in May 1863. Captured at Fort De Russy, Louisiana on March 14, 1864. Exchanged on June 22, 1864. It, however, never reorganized. The men scattered on cavalry duty.

First Commander: E. W. Fuller (Captain)

Field Officer: Edward T. King (Captain)

Assignments: Unattached, District of West Louisiana, Trans-Mississippi Department (May-November 1863)

Unattached, Walker's Division, District of West Louisiana, Trans-Mississippi Department (November 1863-March 1864)

Battles: Red River Campaign (May 10-22, 1864)

Fort De Russy (March 14, 1864)

73. LOUISIANA ST. MARY'S CANNONEERS ARTILLERY BATTERY

See: LOUISIANA 1ST FIELD ARTILLERY BATTERY

74. LOUISIANA SQUIRES' ARTILLERY BATTERY

See: LOUISIANA WASHINGTON ARTILLERY BATTALION, 1ST COMPANY

75. LOUISIANA STEWART'S ARTILLERY BATTERY

See: LOUISIANA POINTE COUPÉE ARTILLERY BATTALION, COMPANY A

76. LOUISIANA THOMPSON'S ARTILLERY BATTERY

See: LOUISIANA GUARD ARTILLERY BATTERY

77. LOUISIANA WASHINGTON ARTILLERY BATTALION

Organization: Organized at New Orleans as a battery in 1838. Mustered into Confederate service for the war with four companies in Lafayette Square, New Orleans on May 26, 1861. A fifth company was organized on March 6, 1862. Captured as part of Walker's artillery column on April 8, 1865.

First Commander: James B. Walton (Major, Colonel)

Field Officers: Benjamin F. Eshleman (Major, Lieutenant Colonel)
Merritt B. Miller (Major)
William M. Owen (Major, Lieutenant Colonel)

Further Reading: Owen, William M., *In Camp and Battle with the Washington Artillery of New Orleans.*
Bartlett, Napier, *A Soldier's Story of the War.*

78. LOUISIANA WASHINGTON ARTILLERY BATTALION, 1ST COMPANY

Organization: Organized at New Orleans in 1838. Mustered into Confederate service for the war in Lafayette Square, New Orleans on May 26, 1861. It was armed with three 6-lb. Smoothbores and two 6-lb. Rifles on July 21, 1861. It was armed with one 10-lb. Parrott and two 3" Rifles from August to December 1862. It was armed with one 12-lb. Napoleon on July 1-3, 1863. It was armed with one 10-lb. Parrott and three 3" Rifles on December 28, 1864. Captured as part of Walker's artillery column on April 8, 1865.

First Commander: Harry M. Isaacson (Captain)

Captain: Edward Owen

Field Officer: Charles W. Squires (Captain, Major, Lieutenant Colonel, Colonel)

Assignments: Early's Brigade, Army of the Potomac (July 1861)
Early's Brigade, 1st Corps, Army of the Potomac (July 1861)
Washington Artillery Battalion, Reserve Artillery, 1st Corps, Army of the Potomac (August-October 1861)
Washington Artillery Battalion, Reserve Artillery, Potomac District, Department of Northern Virginia (October 1861-February 1862)
Washington Artillery Battalion, Potomac District, Department of Northern Virginia (February-March 1862)
Washington Artillery Battalion, Reserve Artillery, Department of Northern Virginia (March-May 1862)
Washington Artillery Battalion, Longstreet's Division, Army of Northern Virginia (June 1862)
Washington Artillery Battalion, Longstreet's Division, 1st Corps, Army of Northern Virginia (June-July 1862)
Washington Artillery Battalion, Artillery Reserve, 1st Corps, Army of Northern Virginia (August 1862-July 1863)
Washington Artillery Battalion, Artillery, 1st Corps, Army of Northern Virginia (July-September 1863)
Washington Artillery Battalion, Department of North Carolina (September 1863)

Washington Artillery Battalion, Walton's Artillery Command, Department of North Carolina (December 1863-May 1864)
Washington Artillery Battalion, Hoke's Division, Department of North Carolina (May 1864)
Washington Artillery Battalion, Hoke's Division, Department of North Carolina and Southern Virginia (May 1864)
Washington Artillery Battalion, Artillery, 3rd Corps, Army of Northern Virginia (June 1864-April 1865)
Battles: Blackburn's Ford [section] (July 18, 1861)
1st Bull Run (July 21, 1861)
Great Falls (September 4, 1861)
Yorktown Siege (April-May 1862)
Seven Pines (May 31-June 1, 1862)
New Bridge (June 5, 1862)
Seven Days Battles (June 25-July 1, 1862)
Mechanicsville (June 26, 1862)
Gaines' Mill (June 27, 1862)
Savage's Station (June 29, 1862)
Frayser's Farm (June 30, 1862)
Malvern Hill (July 1, 1862)
operations *vs*. US shipping on the James River (July 5-7, 1862)
Rappahannock Station and Beverly Ford (August 23, 1862)
2nd Bull Run (August 28-30, 1862)
Chantilly (September 1, 1862)
South Mountain (September 14, 1862)
Antietam (September 17, 1862)
Fredericksburg (December 13, 1862)
Chancellorsville (May 1-4, 1863)
Gettysburg (July 1-3, 1863)
Waynesboro (July 5, 1863)
Williamsport (July 6, 1863)
New Bern Campaign [detachment] (January-February 1864)
Chester Station (May 10, 1864)
Drewry's Bluff (May 16, 1864)
Port Walthall Junction (May 16, 1864)
Cold Harbor (June 1-3, 1864)
Petersburg Siege (June 1864-April 1865)
Petersburg Final Assault (April 2, 1865)
Appomattox Campaign (March-April 1865)
Further Reading: Owen, William M., *In Camp and Battle with the Washington Artillery of New Orleans*. Bartlett, Napier, *A Soldier's Story of the War*.

79. LOUISIANA WASHINGTON ARTILLERY BATTALION, 2ND COMPANY

Organization: Organized at New Orleans in January 1861. Mustered into Confederate service for the war in Lafayette Square, New Orleans on May 26, 1861. It was armed with four 12-lb. Howitzers on July 21, 1861. It was armed with two 12-lb. Howitzers and two 12-lb. Napoleons in August and September 1862. It was armed with four 12-lb. Napoleons on December 13, 1862. It was armed with one 12-lb. Howitzer and two 12-lb. Napoleons on July 1-3, 1863. It was armed with four 12-lb. Napoleons on December 28, 1864. Captured as part of Walker's artillery column on April 8, 1865.

First Commander: Thomas L. Rosser (Captain)

Captain: John B. Richardson

Assignments: Ewell's Brigade, Army of the Potomac (July 1861)

Ewell's Brigade, 1st Corps, Army of the Potomac (July 1861)

Washington Artillery Battalion, Reserve Artillery, 1st Corps, Army of the Potomac (August-October 1861)

Washington Artillery Battalion, Reserve Artillery, Potomac District, Department of Northern Virginia (October 1861-February 1862)

Washington Artillery Battalion, Potomac District, Department of Northern Virginia (February-March 1862)

Washington Artillery Battalion, Reserve Artillery, Department of Northern Virginia (March-May 1862)

Washington Artillery Battalion, Longstreet's Division, Army of Northern Virginia (June 1862)

Washington Artillery Battalion, Longstreet's Division, 1st Corps, Army of Northern Virginia (June-July 1862)

Washington Artillery Battalion, Artillery Reserve, 1st Corps, Army of Northern Virginia (August 1862-July 1863)

Washington Artillery Battalion, Artillery, 1st Corps, Army of Northern Virginia (July-September 1863)

Washington Artillery Battalion, Department of North Carolina (September 1863)

Washington Artillery Battalion, Walton's Artillery Command, Department of North Carolina (December 1863-May 1864)

Washington Artillery Battalion, Hoke's Division, Department of North Carolina (May 1864)

Washington Artillery Battalion, Hoke's Division, Department of North Carolina and Southern Virginia (May 1864)

Washington Artillery Battalion, Artillery, 3rd Corps, Army of Northern Virginia (June 1864-April 1865)

Battles: Blackburn's Ford (July 18, 1861)
1st Bull Run (July 21, 1861)
Lewinsville [section] (September 11, 1861)
Yorktown Siege (April-May 1862)
Ellison's Mill & Mechanicsville [skirmishes] (May 23-24, 1862)
New Bridge [skirmish] (May 24, 1862)
Seven Days Battles (June 25-July 1, 1862)
Mechanicsville (June 26, 1862)
Gaines' Mill (June 27, 1862)
Savage's Station (June 29, 1862)
Frayser's Farm (June 30, 1862)
Malvern Hill (July 1, 1862)
2nd Bull Run (August 28-30, 1862)
Chantilly (September 1, 1862)
South Mountain (September 14, 1862)
Antietam (September 17, 1862)
Fredericksburg (December 13, 1862)
Chancellorsville (May 1-4, 1863)
Gettysburg (July 1-3, 1863)
Waynesboro (July 5, 1863)
Williamsport (July 6, 1863)
New Bern Campaign [detachment] (January-February 1864)
Chester Station (May 10, 1864)
Drewry's Bluff (May 16, 1864)
Port Walthall Junction (May 16, 1864)
Cold Harbor (June 1-3, 1864)
Petersburg Siege (June 1864-April 1865)
Petersburg Final Assault (April 2, 1865)
Appomattox Campaign (March-April 1865)
Further Reading: Owen, William M., *In Camp and Battle with the Washington Artillery of New Orleans*. Bartlett, Napier, *A Soldier's Story of the War.*

80. LOUISIANA WASHINGTON ARTILLERY BATTALION, 3RD COMPANY

Organization: Organized at New Orleans in the spring of 1861. Mustered into Confederate service for the war in Lafayette Square, New Orleans on May 26, 1861. It was armed with three 6-lb. Smoothbores and one 6-lb. Rifles on July 21, 1861. It was armed with two 12-lb. Napoleons from August to December

1862. It was armed with three 12-lb. Napoleons on July 1-3, 1863. It was armed with four 12-lb. Napoleons on December 28, 1864. Captured as part of Walker's artillery column on April 8, 1865.

First Commander: Merritt B. Miller (Captain)

Captain: Andrew Hero, Jr.

Assignments: D. R. Jones' Brigade, Army of the Potomac [section] (July 1861)
Longstreet's Brigade, Army of the Potomac [section] (July 1861)
D. R. Jones' Brigade, 1st Corps, Army of the Potomac [section] (July 1861)
Longstreet's Brigade, 1st Corps, Army of the Potomac [section] (July 1861)
Washington Artillery Battalion, Reserve Artillery, 1st Corps, Army of the Potomac (August-October 1861)
Washington Artillery Battalion, Reserve Artillery, Potomac District, Department of Northern Virginia (October 1861-February 1862)
Washington Artillery Battalion, Potomac District, Department of Northern Virginia (February-March 1862)
Washington Artillery Battalion, Reserve Artillery, Department of Northern Virginia (March-May 1862)
Washington Artillery Battalion, Longstreet's Division, Army of Northern Virginia (June 1862)
Washington Artillery Battalion, Longstreet's Division, 1st Corps, Army of Northern Virginia (June-July 1862)
Washington Artillery Battalion, Artillery Reserve, 1st Corps, Army of Northern Virginia (August 1862-July 1863)
Washington Artillery Battalion, Artillery, 1st Corps, Army of Northern Virginia (July-September 1863)
Washington Artillery Battalion, Department of North Carolina (September 1863)
Washington Artillery Battalion, Walton's Artillery Command, Department of North Carolina (December 1863-May 1864)
Washington Artillery Battalion, Hoke's Division, Department of North Carolina (May 1864)
Washington Artillery Battalion, Hoke's Division, Department of North Carolina and Southern Virginia (May 1864)
Washington Artillery Battalion, Artillery, 3rd Corps, Army of Northern Virginia (June 1864-April 1865)

Battles: Blackburn's Ford [section] (July 18, 1861)
1st Bull Run (July 21, 1861)
Seven Days Battles (June 25-July 1, 1862)
Mechanicsville (June 26, 1862)
Gaines' Mill (June 27, 1862)
Savage's Station (June 29, 1862)

Frayser's Farm (June 30, 1862)
Malvern Hill (July 1, 1862)
Rappahannock Station and Beverly Ford (August 23, 1862)
2nd Bull Run (August 28-30, 1862)
Chantilly (September 1, 1862)
South Mountain (September 14, 1862)
Antietam (September 17, 1862)
Fredericksburg (December 13, 1862)
Chancellorsville (May 1-4, 1863)
Gettysburg (July 1-3, 1863)
Waynesboro (July 5, 1863)
Williamsport (July 6, 1863)
New Bern Campaign [detachment] (January-February 1864)
Chester Station (May 10, 1864)
Drewry's Bluff (May 16, 1864)
Port Walthall Junction (May 16, 1864)
Cold Harbor (June 1-3, 1864)
Petersburg Siege (June 1864-April 1865)
Petersburg Final Assault (April 2, 1865)
Fort Gregg [detachment] (April 2, 1865)
Fort Whitworth [detachment] (April 2, 1865)
Appomattox Campaign (March-April 1865)
Further Reading: Owen, William M., *In Camp and Battle with the Washington Artillery of New Orleans*. Bartlett, Napier, *A Soldier's Story of the War.*

81. LOUISIANA WASHINGTON ARTILLERY BATTALION, 4TH COMPANY

Organization: Organized at New Orleans in the spring of 1861. Mustered into Confederate service for the war in Lafayette Square, New Orleans on May 26, 1861. It was armed with two 6-lb. Smoothbores on July 21, 1861. It was armed with two 12-lb. Howitzers and two 6-lb. Smoothbores in August and September 1862. It was armed with two 12-lb. Howitzers and two 12-lb. Napoleons on December 13, 1862. It was armed with one 12-lb. Howitzer and two 12-lb. Napoleons on July 1-3, 1863. It was armed with three 12-lb. Napoleons and one 10-lb. Parrott on December 28, 1864. Captured as part of Walker's artillery column on April 8, 1865.
First Commander: Benjamin F. Eshleman (Captain)
Captain: Joseph Norcom
Assignments: Reserve Artillery, Army of the Potomac (July 1861)
Reserve Artillery, 1st Corps, Army of the Potomac (July 1861)

Washington Artillery Battalion, Reserve Artillery, 1st Corps, Army of the Potomac (August-October 1861)
Washington Artillery Battalion, Reserve Artillery, Potomac District, Department of Northern Virginia (October 1861-February 1862)
Washington Artillery Battalion, Potomac District, Department of Northern Virginia (February-March 1862)
Washington Artillery Battalion, Reserve Artillery, Department of Northern Virginia (March-May 1862)
Washington Artillery Battalion, Longstreet's Division, Army of Northern Virginia (June 1862)
Washington Artillery Battalion, Longstreet's Division, 1st Corps, Army of Northern Virginia (June-July 1862)
Washington Artillery Battalion, Artillery Reserve, 1st Corps, Army of Northern Virginia (August 1862-July 1863)
Washington Artillery Battalion, Artillery, 1st Corps, Army of Northern Virginia (July-September 1863)
Washington Artillery Battalion, Department of North Carolina (September 1863)
Washington Artillery Battalion, Walton's Artillery Command, Department of North Carolina (December 1863-May 1864)
Washington Artillery Battalion, Hoke's Division, Department of North Carolina (May 1864)
Washington Artillery Battalion, Hoke's Division, Department of North Carolina and Southern Virginia (May 1864)
Washington Artillery Battalion, Artillery, 3rd Corps, Army of Northern Virginia (June 1864-April 1865)
Battles: Blackburn's Ford (July 18, 1861)
1st Bull Run (July 21, 1861)
Seven Days Battles (June 25-July 1, 1862)
Mechanicsville (June 26, 1862)
Gaines' Mill (June 27, 1862)
Savage's Station (June 29, 1862)
Frayser's Farm (June 30, 1862)
Malvern Hill (July 1, 1862)
2nd Bull Run (August 28-30, 1862)
Chantilly (September 1, 1862)
South Mountain (September 14, 1862)
Antietam (September 17, 1862)
Fredericksburg (December 13, 1862)
Chancellorsville (May 1-4, 1863)
Gettysburg (July 1-3, 1863)

Waynesboro (July 5, 1863)
Williamsport (July 6, 1863)
New Bern Campaign [detachment] (January-February 1864)
Chester Station (May 10, 1864)
Drewry's Bluff (May 16, 1864)
Port Walthall Junction (May 16, 1864)
Cold Harbor (June 1-3, 1864)
Petersburg Siege (June 1864-April 1865)
Appomattox Campaign (March-April 1865)
Further Reading: Owen, William M., *In Camp and Battle with the Washington Artillery of New Orleans*. Bartlett, Napier, *A Soldier's Story of the War*.

82. LOUISIANA WASHINGTON ARTILLERY BATTALION, 5TH COMPANY

Organization: Organized for 90 days in Lafayette Square, New Orleans on March 6, 1862. It was armed with two 6-lb. Smoothbores, two 6-lb. Rifles, and two 12-lb. Howitzers on April 6-7, 1862. It was armed with two 6-lb. Smoothbores and two 12-lb. Howitzers on March 29, 1864. Surrendered by Lieutenant Richard Taylor, commanding the Department of Alabama, Mississippi, and East Louisiana, at Citronelle, Alabama on May 4, 1865.
First Commander: W. Irving Hodgson (Captain)
Captain: Cuthbert H. Slocomb
Assignments: Department #1 (March 1862)
Anderson's Brigade, Ruggles'-Cheatham's-Ruggles' Division, 2nd Corps, Army of the Mississippi, Department #2 (March-June 1862)
Anderson's Brigade, 2nd Corps, Army of the Mississippi, Department #2 (June-July 1862)
Anderson's Brigade, Jones' Division, Army of the Mississippi, Department #2 (July-August 1862)
Anderson's-Adams' Brigade, Anderson's Division, 2nd Corps, Army of the Mississippi, Department #2 (August-November 1862)
Adams' Brigade, Anderson's Division, 2nd Corps, Army of Tennessee (November-December 1862)
Adams' Brigade, Breckinridge's Division, 2nd Corps, Army of Tennessee (December 1862-May 1863)
Adams' Brigade, Breckinridge's Division, Department of the West (May-July 1863)
Artillery Battalion, Breckinridge's Division, Department of the West (July 1863)
Artillery Battalion, Breckinridge's Division, Department of Mississippi and East Louisiana (July-August 1863)

Artillery Battalion, Breckinridge's Division, 2nd Corps, Army of Tennessee (August 1863-February 1864)
Cobb's Battalion, Artillery, 2nd Corps, Army of Tennessee (February-April 1864)
Cobb's Battalion, Artillery, 1st Corps, Army of Tennessee (April 1864-January 1865)
Cobb's Artillery Battalion, Right Wing, Defenses of Mobile, Artillery Reserves, etc., District of the Gulf, Department of Alabama, Mississippi, and East Louisiana (March-April 1865)
Cobb's Battalion, Smith's Artillery Regiment, Department of Alabama, Mississippi, and East Louisiana (April-May 1865)
Battles: Shiloh (April 6-7, 1862)
Corinth Campaign (April-June 1862)
Monterey (April 29, 1862)
Farmington (May 9, 1862)
Kentucky Campaign (August-October 1862)
Munfordville (September 17, 1862)
Perryville (October 8, 1862)
Overall's Creek (December 31, 1862)
Murfreesboro (December 31, 1862-January 3, 1863)
Jackson Siege (July 10-17, 1863)
Chickamauga (September 19-20, 1863)
Chattanooga Siege (September-November 1863)
Chattanooga (November 23-25, 1863)
Atlanta Campaign (May-September 1864)
Resaca (May 14-15, 1864)
Dallas (June 25-27, 1864)
Atlanta Siege (July-September 1864)
Franklin (November 30, 1864)
Murfreesboro (December 5-7, 1864)
Nashville (December 15-16, 1864)
Mobile (March 17-April 12, 1865)
Spanish Fort (March 27-April 8, 1865)
Further Reading: Owen, William M., *In Camp and Battle with the Washington Artillery of New Orleans*. Bartlett, Napier, *A Soldier's Story of the War*.

83. LOUISIANA WASHINGTON ARTILLERY BATTALION, 6TH COMPANY

Organization: Organized in April 1862. Disbanded later in 1862. This company does not appear in the *Official Records*.
First Commander: Harmon Doane (Captain)

Assignment: Department #1 (April 1862)
Further Reading: Bartlett, Napier, *A Soldier's Story of the War.*

84. LOUISIANA WATSON ARTILLERY BATTERY

Organization: Organized at New Orleans ca. July 1, 1861. It was armed with four 6-lb. Smoothbores and two 12-lb. Howitzers on April 6-7, 1862. Surrendered at Port Hudson, Louisiana on July 8, 1863. Paroled in July 1863. Never reorganized and the men were assigned to other batteries.
First Commander: Daniel M. Beltzhoover (Captain)
Captain: Allen A. Bursley
Assignments: Department #1 (July-September 1861)
Martin's Brigade, Bowen's Division, 1st Geographical Division, Department #2 (October-December 1861)
Cleburne's Brigade, Hardee's Division, Central Army of Kentucky, Department #2 (February-March 1862)
Bowen's-Helm's Brigade, Reserve Corps, Army of the Mississippi, Department #2 (March-June 1862)
Helm's Brigade, Breckinridge's Division, Department of Southern Mississippi and East Louisiana (June-July 1862)
Bowen's Brigade, District of the Mississippi, Department #2 (July-October 1862)
Bowen's Brigade, Lovell's Division, District of the Mississippi, Army of West Tennessee, Department #2 (October 1862)
Bowen's Brigade, Lovell's-Rust's Division, Lovell's Corps, Army of West Tennessee, Department of Mississippi and East Louisiana (October-December 1862)
Bowen's Brigade, Rust's Division, Lovell's Corps, Army of North Mississippi, Department of Mississippi and East Louisiana (December 1862-January 1863)
Buford's Brigade, 3rd Military District, Department of Mississippi and East Louisiana (March-April 1863)
4th Military District, Department of Mississippi and East Louisiana (April 1863)
Maxey's Brigade, 3rd Military District, Department of Mississippi and East Louisiana (April-May 1863)
Beall's Brigade, 3rd Military District, Department of Mississippi and East Louisiana (May-July 1863)
Battles: Belmont (November 7, 1861)
Shiloh (April 6-7, 1862)
Corinth Campaign (April-June 1862)
Vicksburg Bombardments (May 18-July 27, 1862)

Corinth (October 3-4, 1862)
Tuscumbia River Bridge (October 5, 1862)
Port Hudson Siege (May-July 1863)

85. LOUISIANA WEST'S ARTILLERY BATTERY

See: LOUISIANA 6TH FIELD ARTILLERY BATTERY

86. LOUISIANA WINCHESTER'S ARTILLERY BATTERY

See: LOUISIANA 5TH FIELD ARTILLERY BATTERY

87. LOUISIANA YOIST'S ARTILLERY BATTERY

See: LOUISIANA 6TH FIELD ARTILLERY BATTERY

CAVALRY

88. LOUISIANA 1ST CAVALRY BATTALION, STATE GUARD

Organization: Organized with three companies in March 1863. Mustered in state service at Shreveport on June 12, 1863. Transferred to Confederate service on March 10, 1864. Consolidated with the 2nd Cavalry Battalion, State Guards, and designated as the 8th Cavalry Regiment on October 27, 1864.

First Commander: Benjamin W. Clark (Lieutenant Colonel)

Field Officers: Thomas J. Caldwell (Major)

Robert E. Wyche (Major)

Assignments: Unattached, District of West Louisiana, Trans-Mississippi Department (March 1863-February 1864)

Major's Brigade [temporarily attached], Green's-Wharton's Cavalry Division, District of West Louisiana, Trans-Mississippi Department (April 1864)

Vincent's Cavalry Brigade, District of West Louisiana, Trans-Mississippi Department (August-September 1864)

Vincent's Cavalry Brigade, 1st Corps, Trans-Mississippi Department (September-October 1864)

Battles: Trinity (November 15-16, 1863)

Red River Campaign (May 10-22, 1864)

Mansfield [not engaged] (April 8, 1864)

Monett's Ferry (April 23, 1864)

89. LOUISIANA 1ST (BUCKNER'S) CAVALRY BATTALION

See: ARKANSAS [AND LOUISIANA] 1ST CAVALRY BATTALION

90. LOUISIANA 1ST TRANS-MISSISSIPPI CAVALRY BATTALION

See: CONFEDERATE 1ST TRANS-MISSISSIPPI CAVALRY BATTALION

91. LOUISIANA 1ST CAVALRY REGIMENT

Organization: Organized for the war at Baton Rouge on September 11, 1861. Surrendered by Lieutenant General Richard Taylor, commanding the Department of Alabama, Mississippi, and East Louisiana, at Citronelle, Alabama on May 4, 1865.

First Commander: John S. Scott (Colonel)

Field Officers: Sieb W. Campbell (Major)

James O. Nixon (Lieutenant Colonel)

Gervais Schalter (Major)

John M. Taylor (Major)

Assignments: Department #1 (September-October 1861)

Unattached, Buckner's Division, Central Army of Kentucky, Department #2 (January-February 1862)

Bowen's Brigade, Pillow's Division, Central Army of Kentucky, Department #2 (February-March 1862)

Cavalry, Army of the Mississippi, Department #2 (March-June 1862)

Forrest's Cavalry Brigade, Army of the Mississippi, Department #2 (June-July 1862)

Forrest's Cavalry Brigade, Heth's Division, Department of East Tennessee (July 1862)

Unattached, Heth's Division, Department of East Tennessee (July 1862)

Scott's Cavalry Brigade, Army of Kentucky, Department #2 (August-October 1862)

Scott's Cavalry Brigade, Department of East Tennessee (October-November 1862)

Pegram's Brigade, Wheeler's Cavalry Division, Army of Tennessee (November 1862-January 1863)

Pegram's Cavalry Brigade, Department of East Tennessee (January-April 1863)

Scott's Cavalry Brigade, Army of Tennessee (July-August 1863)

Scott's Brigade, Pegram's Division, Forrest's Cavalry Corps, Army of Tennessee (September-October 1863)

General Headquarters, Army of Tennessee (November 1863-January 1864)

Unattached, Army of Tennessee (January-March 1864)

District of South Mississippi and East Louisiana, Department of Alabama, Mississippi, and East Louisiana (April-June 1864)

Scott's Brigade, W. Adams' Cavalry Division, Department of Alabama, Mississippi, and East Louisiana (June-August 1864)

Scott's Cavalry Brigade, District South of Homochitto, Department of Alabama, Mississippi, and East Louisiana (August-October 1864)

[Sub-]district of Southwest Mississippi and East Louisiana, District of Mississippi and East Louisiana, Department of Alabama, Mississippi, and East Louisiana (November-December 1864)
Scott's Cavalry Brigade, Northern Sub-district of Mississippi, District of Mississippi and East Louisiana, Department of Alabama, Mississippi, and East Louisiana (December 1864-February 1865)
Scott's Cavalry Brigade, District of North Mississippi and West Tennessee, Department of Alabama, Mississippi, and East Louisiana (February-May 1865)
Battles: Granny White's Pike, near Nashville [skirmish] (March 9, 1862)
Corinth Campaign (April-June 1862)
Athens (May 1-2, 1862)
Elk River (May 1-2, 1862)
Kentucky Campaign (August 1862)
Big Hill (August 23, 1862)
Richmond (August 30, 1862)
Munfordville (September 17, 1862)
Murfreesboro (December 31, 1862-January 3, 1863)
Pegram's Kentucky Raid (March 22-April 1, 1863)
Monticello, Kentucky Expedition (April 26-May 12, 1863)
Tullahoma Campaign (June-July 1863)
Scott's Eastern Kentucky Raid (July 25-August 6, 1863)
Lancaster [skirmish] (July 31, 1863)
Chickamauga (September 19-20, 1863)
Chattanooga Siege (September-November 1863)
Chattanooga (November 23-25, 1863)
Mount Pleasant Landing, near Port Hudson (May 15, 1864)
Doyal's Plantation (August 5, 1864)
Thompson's Creek (October 5, 1864)
Bayou Sara [skirmishes] (October 9-10, 1864)
Liberty (November 18, 1864)
Further Reading: Gremillion, Nelson, *Company G, 1st Regiment Louisiana Cavalry, CSA: A Narrative*. Carter, Howell, *A Cavalryman's Reminscences of the Civil War*.

92. LOUISIANA 1ST CAVALRY REGIMENT, PARTISAN RANGERS

See: LOUISIANA 9TH CAVALRY BATTALION, PARTISAN RANGERS

93. LOUISIANA 2ND CAVALRY BATTALION, STATE GUARD

Organization: Organized with seven companies by the mounting of the 1st Infantry Battalion, State Troops (three companies) ca. February 15, 1864.

Transferred to Confederate service on March 10, 1864. Consolidated with the 1st Cavalry Battalion, State Guards, and transferred to Confederate service and designated as the 8th Cavalry Regiment on October 27, 1864.
First Commander: Henry M. Favrot (Lieutenant Colonel)
Field Officer: Samuel McCutcheon (Major)
Assignments: Unattached, District of West Louisiana, Trans-Mississippi Department (April 1864)
Vincent's Cavalry Brigade, District of West Louisiana, Trans-Mississippi Department (August-September 1864)
Vincent's Cavalry Brigade, 1st Corps, Trans-Mississippi Department (September-October 1864)
Battles: Berwick Bay [Company C] [skirmish] (June 23, 1863)
Red River Campaign (May 10-22, 1864)
Mansfield [not engaged] (April 8, 1864)

94. LOUISIANA 2ND CAVALRY REGIMENT

Also Known As: 33rd Cavalry Regiment, Partisan Rangers
Organization: Organized by the increase of Breazeale's Cavalry Battalion, Partisan Rangers, to a regiment ca. September 1, 1862. Surrendered by General E. K. Smith, commanding Trans-Mississippi Department, on May 26, 1865.
First Commander: William G. Vincent (Colonel)
Field Officers: James D. Blair (Major, Lieutenant Colonel)
Winter W. Breazeale (Major, Lieutenant Colonel)
W. Overton Breazeale (Major, Lieutenant Colonel)
S. C. Furman (Major)
James M. Thompson (Major)
James A. McWaters (Lieutenant Colonel)
Assignments: Unattached, District of West Louisiana, Trans-Mississippi Department (September 1862-April 1863)
Green's Cavalry Brigade, District of West Louisiana, Trans-Mississippi Department (June-November 1863)
Unattached, District of West Louisiana, Trans-Mississippi Department (November 1863-May 1864)
Vincent's Cavalry Brigade, District of West Louisiana, Trans-Mississippi Department (August-September 1864)
Vincent's Cavalry Brigade, 1st Corps, Trans-Mississippi Department (September-October 1864)
1st (Vincent's-Brent's) Louisiana Cavalry Brigade, 1st Louisiana Cavalry Division, 1st Corps, Trans-Mississippi Department (December 1864-May 1865)
Battles: Donaldsonville (September 21-25, 1862)
Georgia Landing, near Labadieville (October 27, 1862)

Bayou Teche (January 14, 1863)
Fort Bisland [in reserve] (April 13-14, 1863)
Irish Bend (April 14, 1863)
Brashear City [detachment] (June 23, 1863)
Red River Campaign (May 10-22, 1864)
Henderson's Hill (March 21, 1864)
Mansfield (April 8, 1864)

95. LOUISIANA 2ND (BUSH'S) CAVALRY REGIMENT

See: LOUISIANA 7TH CAVALRY REGIMENT

96. LOUISIANA 3RD CAVALRY BATTALION, STATE GUARD

Organization: Organized in state service with two companies in East Louisiana on June 25, 1864. The battalion was refused transfer into Confederate service by the War Department. This battalion does not appear in the *Official Records*. Disbanded at Alexandria ca. December 1864.
First Commander: James B. Corkern (Major)
Assignments: Scott's Brigade, W. Adams' Cavalry Division, Department of Alabama, Mississippi, and East Louisiana (July-August 1864)
Scott's Cavalry Brigade, District South of Homochitto, Department of Alabama, Mississippi, and East Louisiana (August-September 1864)
Unattached, 1st Corps, Trans-Mississippi Department (December 1864)

97. LOUISIANA 3RD (HARRISON'S) CAVALRY REGIMENT

Organization: Organized by the increase of the 15th Cavalry Battalion to a regiment in the fall of 1863. Surrendered by General E. K. Smith, commanding Trans-Mississippi Department, on May 26, 1865.
First Commander: Isaac F. Harrison (Colonel)
Field Officers: E. S. McCall (Major)
Francis W. Moore (Lieutenant Colonel)
William R. Purvis (Lieutenant Colonel)
Assignments: District of West Louisiana, Trans-Mississippi Department (November 1863)
Harrison's Cavalry Brigade, District of West Louisiana, Trans-Mississippi Department (November 1863-September 1864)
Harrison's Cavalry Brigade, 1st Corps, Trans-Mississippi Department (September-October 1864)
3rd (Harrison's-Gray's) Louisiana Cavalry Brigade, 1st Louisiana Cavalry Division, 1st Corps, Trans-Mississippi Department (December 1864-May 1865)
Battles: Red River Campaign (May 10-22, 1864)

Fort DeRussy [detachment Company H] (March 14, 1864)
Bayou Des Cedars (April 17, 1864)
Hadnot's Plantation (May 1, 1864)

98. LOUISIANA 3RD (PARGOUD'S) CAVALRY REGIMENT

Organization: Organized by the addition of four independent companies to the 13th Cavalry Battalion at Monroe in November 1862. Lieutenant Colonel Chambliss, however, refused to comply and the 13th Cavalry Battalion was restored in February 1863. This effectively broke up the regiment.
First Commander: John F. Pargoud (Colonel)
Field Officers: Richard L. Capers (Major)
Samuel L. Chambliss (Lieutenant Colonel)
Assignment: Sub-district of North Louisiana, District of West Louisiana, Trans-Mississippi Department (November 1862-February 1863)

99. LOUISIANA 3RD (WINGFIELD'S) CAVALRY REGIMENT

Organization: Organized by the redesignation of the 9th Cavalry Battalion, Partisan Rangers ca. September 1864. Surrendered by Lieutenant General Richard Taylor, commanding the Department of Alabama, Mississippi, and East Louisiana, at Citronelle, Alabama on May 4, 1865.
First Commander: James H. Wingfield (Colonel)
Field Officers: Obediah P. Amacker (Lieutenant Colonel)
Edwin A. Scott (Major)
Assignments: [Sub-]district of Southwest Mississippi and East Louisiana, District of Mississippi and East Louisiana, Department of Alabama, Mississippi, and East Louisiana (September-December 1864)
Scott's Cavalry Brigade, Northern Sub-district of Mississippi, District of Mississippi and East Louisiana, Department of Alabama, Mississippi, and East Louisiana (December 1864-February 1865)
Scott's Cavalry Brigade, District of North Mississippi and West Tennessee, Department of Alabama, Mississippi, and East Louisiana (February-May 1865)
Battles: Bayou Sara [skirmishes] (October 9-10, 1864)
Jackson (October 5, 1864)

100. LOUISIANA 4TH CAVALRY REGIMENT

Organization: Organized by the increase of the 19th Cavalry Battalion to a regiment ca. January 1864. Surrendered by General E. K. Smith, commanding Trans-Mississippi Department, on May 26, 1865.
First Commander: Archibald J. McNeill (Colonel)
Field Officer: Matt. F. Johnson (Lieutenant Colonel)

Assignments: Harrison's Cavalry Brigade, Sub-district of North Louisiana, District of West Louisiana, Trans-Mississippi Department (January-April 1864)

Harrison's Louisiana Cavalry Brigade, District of West Louisiana, Trans-Mississippi Department (August-September 1864)

Harrison's Cavalry Brigade, 1st Corps, Trans-Mississippi Department (September-October 1864)

3rd (Harrison's-Gray's) Louisiana Cavalry Brigade, 1st Louisiana Cavalry Division, 1st Corps, Trans-Mississippi Department (December 1864-May 1865)

Battle: Red River Campaign (May 10-22, 1864)

101. LOUISIANA 4TH (BUSH'S) CAVALRY REGIMENT

See: LOUISIANA 7TH CAVALRY REGIMENT

102. LOUISIANA 5TH CAVALRY REGIMENT

Organization: Organized by the increase of the 13th Cavalry Battalion to a regiment on February 20, 1864. Surrendered by General E. K. Smith, commanding Trans-Mississippi Department, on May 26, 1865.

First Commander: Richard L. Capers (Colonel)

Field Officers: James H. Capers (Lieutenant Colonel)

W. H. Corbin (Major)

John S. Young (Major, Lieutenant Colonel)

Assignments: Harrison's Louisiana Cavalry Brigade, Sub-district of North Louisiana, District of West Louisiana, Trans-Mississippi Department (February-September 1864)

Harrison's Cavalry Brigade, 1st Corps, Trans-Mississippi Department (September-October 1864)

3rd (Harrison's-Gray's) Louisiana Cavalry Brigade, 1st Louisiana Cavalry Division, 1st Corps, Trans-Mississippi Department (December 1864-May 1865)

103. LOUISIANA 6TH CAVALRY REGIMENT

Organization: Organized by the increase of William Harrison's Cavalry Battalion to a regiment ca. August 1864. Surrendered by General E. K. Smith, commanding Trans-Mississippi Department, on May 26, 1865.

First Commander: William Harrison (Colonel)

Field Officers: William M. Lacy (Lieutenant)

William B. Denson (Lieutenant Colonel)

William J. Scott (Major)

Assignments: Vincent's Cavalry Brigade, District of West Louisiana, Trans-Mississippi Department (August-September 1864)

Vincent's Cavalry Brigade, 1st Corps, Trans-Mississippi Department (September-October 1864)

3rd (Harrison's-Gray's) Louisiana Cavalry Brigade, 1st Louisiana Cavalry Division, 1st Corps, Trans-Mississippi Department (December 1864-May 1865)

104. LOUISIANA 7TH CAVALRY REGIMENT

Also Known As: 2nd Cavalry Regiment, 4th Cavalry Regiment

Organization: Organized as the 4th Cavalry Regiment at Moundville on March 13, 1864 . Reorganized as the 7th Cavalry Regiment in October 1864. Surrendered by General E. K. Smith, commanding Trans-Mississippi Department, on May 26, 1865.

First Commander: Louis Bush (Colonel)

Field Officers: James D. Blair (Lieutenant Colonel)

Louis A. Bringier (Lieutenant Colonel)

William Mouton (Major)

A. L. Pitzer (Major)

Assignments: Unattached, District of West Louisiana, Trans-Mississippi Department (March-May 1864)

Vincent's Louisiana Cavalry Brigade, District of West Louisiana, Trans-Mississippi Department (August-September 1864)

Vincent's Cavalry Brigade, 1st Corps, Trans-Mississippi Department (September-October 1864)

1st (Vincent's-Brent's) Louisiana Cavalry Brigade, 1st Louisiana Cavalry Division, 1st Corps, Trans-Mississippi Department (December 1864-May 1865)

Battles: Red River Campaign (May 10-22, 1864)

Crump's Hill (April 2, 1864)

Wilson's Farm (April 7, 1864)

105. LOUISIANA 8TH CAVALRY REGIMENT

Organization: Organized by the consolidation of the 1st and 2nd Cavalry Battalions, State Guards, to a regiment on October 27, 1864. Surrendered by General E. K. Smith, commanding Trans-Mississippi Department, on May 26, 1865.

First Commander: Benjamin W. Clark (Lieutenant Colonel)

Field Officers: Thomas J. Caldwell (Major)

Samuel McCutcheon (Lieutenant Colonel)

Assignment: 1st (Vincent's-Brent's) Louisiana Cavalry Brigade, 1st Louisiana Cavalry Division, 1st Corps, Trans-Mississippi Department (October 1864-May 1865)

106. LOUISIANA 9TH CAVALRY BATTALION, PARTISAN RANGERS

Also Known As: 1st Cavalry Regiment, Partisan Rangers

Organization: Organized as the 1st Cavalry Regiment, Partisan Rangers at Camp Moore on May 28, 1862. Designated as the 9th Cavalry Battalion, Partisan Rangers when several companies were disbanded in August 1862. The disbanded companies were reorganized at Camp Moore in early 1863. Surrendered at Port Hudson, Louisiana on July 8, 1863. Paroled in July 1863. Exchanged in the fall of 1863. Redesignated as the 3rd (Wingfield's) Cavalry Regiment ca. September 1864.

First Commander: James H. Wingfield (Lieutenant Colonel)

Field Officers: James DeBaun (Major)

Fred N. Ogden (Major [temporarily])

Assignments: Department of Southern Mississippi and East Louisiana (June-July 1862)

1st Sub-district, District of the Mississippi, Department #2 (July-August 1862)

Unattached, Breckinridge's Command, District of the Mississippi, Department #2 (August 1862)

1st Sub-district, District of the Mississippi, Department #2 (August-October 1862)

Department of Mississippi and East Louisiana (October 1862)

Unattached, 3rd Military District, Department of Mississippi and East Louisiana (October 1862-July 1863)

Logan's-Griffith's-W. Adams' Brigade, Jackson's Division, Lee's Cavalry Corps, Department of Mississippi and East Louisiana (November 1863-January 1864)

W. Adams' Brigade, Jackson's Division, Lee's Cavalry Corps, Department of Alabama, Mississippi, and East Louisiana (January-February 1864)

District of Southwest Mississippi and East Louisiana, Department of Alabama, Mississippi, and East Louisiana (February-March 1864)

W. Adams' Brigade, Jackson's Division, Lee's Cavalry Corps, Department of Alabama, Mississippi, and East Louisiana (March 1864)

District of Southwest Mississippi and East Louisiana, Department of Alabama, Mississippi, and East Louisiana (April-May 1864)

Scott's Brigade, W. Adams' Cavalry Division, Department of Alabama, Mississippi, and East Louisiana (May-August 1864)

Scott's Cavalry Brigade, District South of Homochitto, Department of Alabama, Mississippi, and East Louisiana (August-September 1864)

Battles: Amite River [skirmish] (July 24, 1862)

Baton Rouge (August 5, 1862)

Baton Rouge [skirmish] (August 20, 1862)

Bayou Bonfuca (November 21, 1862)

Port Hudson Bombardment (March 14, 1863)

Plains Store [skirmish] [detachment] (March 14, 1863)

Grierson's Raid (April 17-May 2, 1863)

Wall's Bridge (May 1, 1863)

Thompson's Creek [skirmish] (May 25, 1863)

Sandy Creek [skirmish] (May 25, 1863)

Port Hudson Siege (May-July 1863)

Jackson [skirmishes] (July 5-7, 1864)

Benton's Ferry, Amite River [four companies] (July 25, 1864)

107. LOUISIANA 10TH CAVALRY BATTALION

See: LOUISIANA 18TH CAVALRY BATTALION

108. LOUISIANA 13TH CAVALRY BATTALION, PARTISAN RANGERS

Organization: Organized with six companies by the increase of Bayliss' Cavalry Battalion, Partisan Rangers at Monroe on August 26, 1862. Consolidated with four independent companies and designated as the 3rd (Pargoud's) Cavalry Regiment in November 1862. However, Lieutenant Colonel Chambliss refused to comply and the battalion was restored to its official independent status in February 1863. Subsequently merged into the 5th Cavalry Regiment on February 20, 1864.

First Commander: Samuel L. Chambliss (Major, Lieutenant Colonel)

Field Officers: James H. Capers (Major)

Richard L. Capers (Major, Lieutenant Colonel)

Assignments: District of West Louisiana, Trans-Mississippi Department (August-September 1862)

Unattached, District of West Louisiana, Trans-Mississippi Department (February-October 1863)

Harrison's Cavalry Brigade, Sub-district of North Louisiana, District of West Louisiana, Trans-Mississippi Department (October 1863-February 1864)

Battles: Lake Providence [skirmish] (February 10, 1863)

Caledonia and Pin Hook [skirmishes] (May 10, 1863)

Lake Providence (June 9, 1863)

109. LOUISIANA 15TH CAVALRY BATTALION

Organization: Organized at Monroe with seven companies on September 26, 1862. Company A was formerly 1st Company A, Wirt Adams'-Wood's Mississippi Cavalry Regiment. Increased to a regiment and designated as the 3rd (Harrison's) Cavalry Regiment in the fall of 1863.

First Commander: Isaac F. Harrison (Major, Lieutenant Colonel)

Field Officer: E. S. McCall (Major)

Assignments: Sub-district of North Louisiana, District of West Louisiana, Trans-Mississippi Department (September 1862-January 1863)

Unattached, District of West Louisiana, Trans-Mississippi Department (January-November 1863)

Battles: Dallas (December 25-26, 1862)

Roundaway Bayou, near Richmond (March 31, 1863)

Richmond and Bayou Vidal (April 4, 1863)

James' Plantation, near New Carthage (April 6, 1863)

Choctaw Bayou (April 28, 1863)

Vicksburg Campaign (May-July 1863)

Fort Beauregard (May 10-11, 1863)

Richmond [detachment] (June 6, 1863)

Lake St. Joseph [Company A] (June 4, 1863)

Richmond [detachment] (June 6, 1863)

110. LOUISIANA 18TH CAVALRY BATTALION

Organization: Organized with nine companies at Clinton ca. January 25, 1864. Disbanded with six companies being transferred to Powers' Confederate Cavalry Regiment and two companies to Ogden's Cavalry Battalion in March 1864. Reorganized by the assignment of the seven Louisiana companies of Powers' Confederate Cavalry Regiment on November 21, 1864, per S.O. #276, Adjutant and Inspector General's Office. Surrendered by Lieutenant General Richard Taylor, commanding the Department of Alabama, Mississippi, and East Louisiana, at Citronelle, Alabama on May 4, 1865.

First Commander: Haley M. Carter (Lieutenant Colonel)

Field Officer: Henry N. Sherburne (Major)

Assignments: District of South Mississippi and East Louisiana, Department of Alabama, Mississippi, and East Louisiana (January-March 1864)

Sub-district of Southwest Mississippi, District of Mississippi and East Louisiana, Department of Alabama, Mississippi, and East Louisiana (November-December 1864)

Scott's Cavalry Brigade, Northern Sub-district of Mississippi, District of Mississippi and East Louisiana, Department of Alabama, Mississippi, and East Louisiana (December 1864-February 1865)

Scott's Cavalry Brigade, District of North Mississippi and West Tennessee, Department of Alabama, Mississippi, and East Louisiana (February-May 1865)

Battle: Pickens County [skirmish] (April 6, 1865)

111. LOUISIANA 19TH CAVALRY BATTALION

Organization: Organized with six companies ca. September 1863. Increased to a regiment and designated as the 4th Cavalry Regiment ca. January 1864.

First Commander: Archibald J. McNeill (Major)

Field Officer: Matt. F. Johnson (Major)

Assignment: Harrison's Cavalry Brigade, Sub-district of North Louisiana, District of West Louisiana, Trans-Mississippi Department (November-December 1863)

112. LOUISIANA 33RD CAVALRY REGIMENT, PARTISAN RANGERS

See: LOUISIANA 2ND CAVALRY REGIMENT

113. LOUISIANA BAYLISS CAVALRY BATTALION, PARTISAN RANGERS

Organization: Organized with two companies on June 27, 1862. Increased to six companies and designated as the 13th Cavalry Battalion, Partisan Rangers at Monroe on August 26, 1862. This battalion does not appear in the *Official Records*.

First Commander: W. H. Bayliss (Major)

Assignments: Trans-Mississippi Department (June-August 1862)

District of West Louisiana, Trans-Mississippi Department (August 1862)

114. LOUISIANA BREAZEALE'S CAVALRY BATTALION, PARTISAN RANGERS

Organization: Organized with six companies at Natchitoches ca. July 27, 1862. Mustered into Confederate service at Natchitoches on August 21, 1862. Increased to a regiment and designated as the 2nd Cavalry Regiment ca. September 1, 1862.

First Commander: Winter W. Breazeale (Major)

Assignment: Unattached, District of West Louisiana, Trans-Mississippi Department (July-September 1862)

115. LOUISIANA CAGE'S CAVALRY BATTALION

See: LOUISIANA MILES' LEGION CAVALRY BATTALION

116. LOUISIANA GOBER'S CAVALRY REGIMENT

See: LOUISIANA GOBER'S MOUNTED INFANTRY REGIMENT

117. LOUISIANA HARRISON'S W. CAVALRY BATTALION

Organization: Organized with six companies ca. December 1863. Increased to a regiment and designated as the 6th Cavalry Regiment ca. August 1864.
First Commander: William Harrison (Lieutenant Colonel)
Field Officer: William B. Denson (Major)
Assignment: Unattached, District of West Louisiana, Trans-Mississippi Department (April-August 1864)
Battle: Red River Campaign (May 10-22, 1864)

118. LOUISIANA MILES' LEGION CAVALRY BATTALION

Organization: Organized with three, formerly independent, companies in mid-May 1863. Became Companies E, D, and G, respectively, 14th Confederate Cavalry Regiment on September 14, 1863. However, these companies tended to serve separately from the rest of the regiment. [NOTE: See also Louisiana Miles' Legion Infantry Battalion; Louisiana Gibson's Artillery Battery; and Louisiana 2nd Siege Artillery Battery.]
First Commander: John B. Cage (Major [acting])
Field Officer: James T. Coleman (Major)
Assignments: Department #1 (May-June 1862)
Department of Southern Mississippi and East Louisiana (June-July 1862)
1st Sub-district, District of the Mississippi, Department #2 (July-October 1862)
Department of Mississippi and East Louisiana (October 1862)
3rd Military District, Department of Mississippi and East Louisiana (October 1862)
Maxey's Brigade, 3rd Military District, Department of Mississippi and East Louisiana (December 1862-February 1863)
Miles' Brigade, 3rd Military District, Department of Mississippi and East Louisiana (March 1863)
Cavalry, 3rd Military District, Department of Mississippi and East Louisiana (March-September 1863)
Logan's Cavalry Brigade, Department of Mississippi and East Louisiana (September 1863)
Battles: Port Hudson Siege (May-July 1863)
Bayou Manchac, Amite River [one company] (March 26, 1863)
Pretty Creek [skirmish] (June 3, 1863)
Grierson's Raid (April 17-May 2, 1863)
Jackson [skirmish] (August 3, 1863)

Further Reading: Bergeron, Arthur, Jr. and Lawrence L. Hewitt, *Miles' Legion: A History and Roster.*

119. LOUISIANA OGDEN'S CAVALRY BATTALION

Organization: Organized temproarily with three Louisiana and three Mississippi companies at Clinton on June 6, 1864. Two additional Louisiana companies served with the battalion from time to time. Broken up with one Louisiana company assigned to Ogden's [new] Cavalry Regiment and two other Louisiana companies assigned to the 18th Cavalry Battalion in January 1865.

First Commander: Frederick N. Ogden (Major, Lieutenant Colonel)

Field Officer: B. F. Bryan (Major)

Assignments: Scott's Brigade, W. Adams' Cavalry Division, Department of Alabama, Mississippi, and East Louisiana (June-August 1864)

Scott's Cavalry Brigade, District South of Homochitto, Department of Alabama, Mississippi, and East Louisiana (August-October 1864)

Sub-district of Southwest Mississippi and East Louisiana, District of Mississippi and East Louisiana, Department of Alabama, Mississippi, and East Louisiana (October-December 1864)

Scott's Cavalry Brigade, District of North Mississippi and East Louisiana, Department of Alabama, Mississippi, and East Louisiana (December 1864-January 1865)

Battles: Jackson [skirmishes] (July 5-7, 1864)

Clinton (November 15, 1864)

Liberty (November 18, 1864)

120. LOUISIANA OGDEN'S CAVALRY REGIMENT

Organization: Organized by the assignment of one company from Ogden's Cavalry Battalion, four companies from the 14th Confederate Cavalry Regiment, three companies from Gober's Mounted Infantry Regiment, and two new companies to form a regiment in January 1865. Companies D, E, G, and H, 14th Confederate Cavalry Regiment became Companies A, I, C, and E, respectively, of this regiment. Surrendered by Lieutenant General Richard Taylor, commanding the Department of Alabama, Mississippi, and East Louisiana, at Citronelle, Alabama on May 4, 1865.

First Commander: Frederick N. Ogden (Colonel)

Assignments: Scott's Cavalry Brigade, District of North Mississippi and East Louisiana, Department of Alabama, Mississippi, and East Louisiana (January-February 1865)

Sub-district of Southeastern Louisiana, District of Mississippi and East Louisiana, Department of Alabama, Mississippi, and East Louisiana [Companies G & H] (January-February 1865)

Scott's Cavalry Brigade, District of North Mississippi and West Tennessee, Department of Alabama, Mississippi, and East Louisiana (February-May 1865)

Sub-district of Southeastern Louisiana, District of Southern Mississippi and East Louisiana, Department of Alabama, Mississippi, and East Louisiana [Companies G & H] (February-April 1865)

121. LOUISIANA ORLEANS LIGHT HORSE CAVALRY COMPANY

Organization: Organized at New Orleans in 1861. Mustered into Confederate service on March 22, 1862. Surrendered by General Joseph E. Johnston at Durham Station, Orange County, North Carolina on April 26, 1865.

First Commander: J. McD. Taylor (Captain)

Captains: Thomas L. Leeds

W. Alexander Gordon

Leeds Greenleaf

Assignments: Department #1 (December 1861-March 1862)

Escort, 1st Corps, Army of the Mississippi, Department #2 (March-July 1862)

Escort, Army of the Mississippi, Department #2 (July-August 1862)

Escort, Right Wing, Army of the Mississippi, Department #2 (August-November 1862)

Escort, 1st Corps, Army of Tennessee (November 1862-October 1863)

Escort, Department of Mississippi and East Louisiana (December 1863-January 1864)

Escort, Department of Alabama, Mississippi, and East Louisiana (January-May 1864)

Escort, Army of Mississippi (May-July 1864)

Escort, 3rd Corps, Army of Tennessee (July 1864-April 1865)

Battles: Shiloh (April 6-7, 1862)

Perryville (October 8, 1862)

Murfreesboro (December 31, 1862-January 3, 1863)

Tullahoma Campaign (June-July 1863)

Chickamauga (September 19-20, 1863)

Meridian Campaign (February-March 1864)

Atlanta Campaign (May-September 1864)

Atlanta Siege (July-September 1864)

Franklin (November 30, 1864)

Nashville (December 15-16, 1864)

Mobile (March 17-April 12, 1865)

122. LOUISIANA [AND MISSISSIPPI] POWERS' CAVALRY REGIMENT

See: CONFEDERATE POWERS' CAVALRY REGIMENT

123. LOUISIANA RED RIVER SCOUTS CAVALRY BATTALION

Also Known As: Louisiana Red River Sharpshooters Battalion, Louisiana Steamboat Cavalry Battalion

Organization: Organized with two companies recruited from vessels plying the Red River at Shreveport in late 1863. A third company was subsequently assigned. No field officers were ever appointed. Surrendered by General E. K. Smith, commanding Trans-Mississippi Department, on May 26, 1865.

Assignments: Unattched, District of West Louisiana, Trans-Mississippi Department (November 1863-April 1865)

Unattached, District of Arkansas and West Louisiana, Trans-Mississippi Department (April-May 1865)

Battles: Red River Campaign (May 10-22, 1864)

Fort DeRussy [detachment Company B] (March 14, 1864)

124. LOUISIANA STEAMBOAT CAVALRY BATTALION

See: LOUISIANA RED RIVER SCOUTS CAVALRY BATTALION

125. LOUISIANA WILSON RANGERS CAVALRY COMPANY, MILITIA

Organization: Called into service on March 1, 1862. Mustered out later in 1862.

First Commander: Moore (Captain)

Assignment: 2nd (Tracy's) Brigade, Louisiana State Troops, Department #1 (March-May 1862)

Battle: New Orleans [not engaged] (April 18-25, 1862)

INFANTRY

126. LOUISIANA 1ST INFANTRY BATTALION

Organization: Organized with five companies at Pensacola, Florida on April 16, 1861. It was originally attached to the 1st Infantry Regiment Regulars. Mustered into Confederate service at Richmond, Virginia on June 11, 1861. A sixth company was assigned July 1861. Disbanded on May 1, 1862. Company D was assigned to the 1st Infantry Regiment.

First Commander: Charles D. Dreux (Lieutenant Colonel)

Field Officers: James H. Beard (Major)

Nicholas H. Rightor (Major, Lieutenant Colonel)

Assignments: Pensacola (April-May 1861)

Department of the Peninsula (June-October 1861)

Williamsburg and Spratley's [B. S. Ewell's Command], Department of the Peninsula (October 1861)

Griffith's Brigade, Magruder's Division, Magruder's Command, Department of Northern Virginia (April-May 1862)

Griffith's Brigade, Magruder's Division, Army of Northern Virginia (May 1862)

Battles: near Newport News (July 5, 1861)

Operations on Back River (July 24, 1861)

Young's Mill (October 21, 1861)

Yorktown Siege (April-May 1862)

Lee's Mill (April 5, 1862)

Further Reading: Meynier, A., *Life and Military Services of Colonel Charles D. Dreux.*

127. LOUISIANA 1ST SPECIAL INFANTRY BATTALION

Also Known As: 2nd Infantry Battalion

Nickname: Louisiana Tigers

Organization: Organized with four companies for the war on May 25, 1861. Battalion organization completed at Camp Moore on June 5, 1861. Mustered into Confederate service on June 6, 1862. Company E assigned on September 1, 1861. Mustered in for the war on June 9, 1861. Broken up, as unmanageable, on August 21, 1862.

First Commander: Chatham R. Wheat (Major)

Field Officer: Robert A. Harris (Major)

Assignments: Evans' Brigade, Army of the Potomac (July 1861)

Evans' Brigade, 1st Corps, Army of the Potomac (July 1861)

W. H. T. Walker's-Taylor's Brigade, 1st Corps, Army of the Potomac (July-October 1861)

Taylor's Brigade, E. K. Smith's Division, 1st Corps, Potomac District, Department of Northern Virginia (October 1861-January 1862)

Taylor's Brigade, E. K. Smith's-Ewell's Division, Potomac District, Department of Northern Virginia (January-March 1862)

Taylor's Brigade, Ewell's Division, Department of Northern Virginia (March-May 1862)

Taylor's Brigade, Ewell's Division, Valley District, Department of Northern Virginia (May-June 1862)

Taylor's Brigade, Ewell's Division, 2nd Corps, Army of Northern Virginia (June-July 1862)

Battles: 1st Bull Run (July 21, 1861)

Shenandoah Valley Campaign (May-June 1862)

Somerville Heights [skirmish] [two companies] (May 7, 1862)

Front Royal (May 23, 1862)

Middletown (May 24, 1862)

1st Winchester [not engaged] (May 25, 1862)

Mount Carmel (June 1, 1862)

Port Republic (June 9, 1862)

Seven Days Battles (June 25-July 1, 1862)

Gaines' Mill (June 27, 1862)

White Oak Swamp (June 30, 1862)

Malvern Hill (July 1, 1862)

Seneca, Potomac River [skirmish] (June 28, 1863)

Further Reading: Jones, Terry L., *Lee's Tigers: The Louisiana Infantry in the Army of Northern Virginia.*

128. LOUISIANA 1ST ZOUAVES INFANTRY BATTALION

Nicknames: Confederate States Zouaves Battalion, Coppens' Zouaves, Louisiana Regiment of Zouaves and Chasseurs

Organization: Organized with six companies at Pensacola, Florida on March 27, 1861. Company E became Company A, 12th Heavy Artillery Battalion in August 1862. Companies B and C, 7th Infantry Battalion were assigned to this battalion in May 1862. Reorganized on November 10, 1862. Surrendered by General Robert E. Lee, commanding the Army of Northern Virginia, on April 9, 1865.

First Commander: George A. Gaston Coppens (Lieutenant Colonel)

Field Officers: Marie A. Coppens (Lieutenant Colonel)

Fulgence De Bordenave (Major)

Waldhemar Hyllestad (Major)

Assignments: Pensacola, Florida (May-June 1861)

Department of the Peninsula (June-October 1861)

Hunt's Brigade, Department of the Peninsula (October 1861)

Rains' Division, Department of the Peninsula (January-February 1862)

Pryor's Brigade, Longstreet's Division, Army of Northern Virginia (June 1862)

Pryor's Brigade, Longstreet's Division, 1st Corps, Army of Northern Virginia (June-July 1862)

2nd Louisiana Brigade, McLaws' Division, 1st Corps, Army of Northern Virginia (July 1862)

2nd Louisiana Brigade, A. P. Hill's Division, 2nd Corps, Army of Northern Virginia (July 1862)

2nd Louisiana Brigade, Jackson's Division, 2nd Corps, Army of Northern Virginia (August-September 1862)

Department of Henrico (December 1862-August 1863)

Unattached, Ransom's Division, Department of Richmond (August-September 1863)

Unattached, Department of North Carolina (December 1863-May 1864)

1st Military District, Department of North Carolina and Southern Virginia (August-September 1864)

Garnett's Brigade, 1st Military District, Department of North Carolina and Southern Virginia (September 1864-April 1865)

Battles: Yorktown Siege (April-May 1862)

Williamsburg (May 5, 1862)

Seven Pines (May 31-June 1, 1862)

Seven Days Battles (June 25-July 1, 1862)

Gaines' Mill (June 27, 1862)

Frayser's Farm (June 30, 1862)

2nd Bull Run (August 28-30, 1862)

Harpers Ferry (September 12-15, 1862)

Antietam (September 17, 1862)

Petersburg Siege (June 1864-April 1865)

Hicksford (December 7-12, 1864)

Further Reading: Jones, Terry L., *Lee's Tigers: The Louisiana Infantry in the Army of Northern Virginia.*

129. LOUISIANA 1ST INFANTRY BATTALION, STATE TROOPS

Organization: Organized with two companies at Shreveport on May 7, 1863. Company C was assigned on June 29, 1863. Disbanded ca. February 15, 1864 and the men were assigned to the 2nd Cavalry Battalion, State Guards.

First Commander: William H. Terrell (Major)

Assignment: District of West Louisiana, Trans-Mississippi Department (May 1863-May 1864)

130. LOUISIANA 1ST INFANTRY REGIMENT

Organization: Organized at New Orleans on April 25, 1861. Mustered into Confederate service for 12 months on April 28, 1861. Company B became the Louisiana Guard Artillery Battery on July 21, 1861. Reorganized for the war on April 30, 1862. Field consolidation with the 14th Infantry Regiment from September 1864 to April 9, 1865. Surrendered at Appomattox Court House, Virginia on April 9, 1865.

First Commander: Albert G. Blanchard (Colonel)

Field Officers: Charles E. Cormier (Major)

Samuel R. Harrison (Major, Colonel)

James Nelligan (Major, Lieutenant Colonel, Colonel)

Michael Nolan (Lieutenant Colonel)

William R. Shivers (Major, Lieutenant Colonel, Colonel)

William G. Vincent (Lieutenant Colonel, Colonel)

Edward D. Willett (Major)

James C. Wise (Major)

Assignments: Department of Norfolk (May-September 1861)

Blanchard's Brigade, Department of Norfolk (September 1861-April 1862)

Blanchard's-Wright's Brigade, Huger's-R. H. Anderson's Division, Army of Northern Virginia (April-July 1862)

Wright's Brigade, R. H. Anderson's Division, 1st Corps, Army of Northern Virginia (July 1862)

2nd Louisiana Brigade, McLaws' Division, 1st Corps, Army of Northern Virginia (July 1862)

2nd Louisiana Brigade, A. P. Hill's Division, 2nd Corps, Army of Northern Virginia (July 1862)

2nd Louisiana Brigade, Jackson's-Johnson's Division, 2nd Corps, Army of Northern Virginia (August 1862-May 1864)

Consolidated Louisiana Brigade, Early's-Gordon's Division, 2nd Corps, Army of Northern Virginia (May-June 1864)

Consolidated Louisiana Brigade, Gordon's Division, Valley District, Department of Northern Virginia (June-December 1864)

Consolidated Louisiana Brigade, Gordon's Division, 2nd Corps, Army of Northern Virginia (December 1864-April 1865)

Battles: Seven Pines (May 31-June 1, 1862)
Seven Days Battles (June 25-July 1, 1862)
King's School House (June 25, 1862)
Malvern Hill (July 1, 1862)
2nd Bull Run (August 28-30, 1862)
Antietam (September 17, 1862)
Fredericksburg (December 13, 1862)
Chancellorsville (May 1-4, 1863)
2nd Winchester (June 14-15, 1863)
Gettysburg (July 1-3, 1863)
Bristoe Campaign (October 1863)
Mine Run Campaign (November-December 1863)
Payne's Farm (November 27, 1863)
The Wilderness (May 5-6, 1864)
Spotsylvania Court House (May 8-21, 1864)
North Anna (May 23-26, 1864)
Cold Harbor (June 1-3, 1864)
Lynchburg Campaign (May-June 1864)
Monocacy (July 9, 1864)
Kernstown (July 24, 1864)
Shepherdstown (August 25, 1864)
3rd Winchester (September 19, 1864)
Fisher's Hill (September 22, 1864)
Cedar Creek (October 19, 1864)
Petersburg Siege [from December] (June 1864-April 1865)
Hatcher's Run (February 5-7, 1865)
Sayler's Creek (April 6, 1865)
Fort Stedman (March 25, 1865)
Petersburg Final Assault (April 2, 1865)
Appomattox Court House (April 9, 1865)

Further Reading: Jones, Terry L., *Lee's Tigers: The Louisiana Infantry in the Army of Northern Virginia.*

131. LOUISIANA 1ST INFANTRY REGIMENT, REGULARS

Organization: Organized in state service on February 5, 1861. Mustered into Confederate service on March 13, 1861. Served as heavy artillery in the summer of 1863. Field consolidation with the 8th Arkansas Infantry Regiment in September and October 1863. Field consolidation with the 16th and 20th Infantry Regiments from February to May 4, 1865. Surrendered by Lieutenant

General Richard Taylor, commanding the Department of Alabama, Mississippi, and East Louisiana, at Meridian, Mississippi on May 4, 1865.

First Commander: Adley H. Gladden (Colonel)

Field Officers: Daniel W. Adams (Lieutenant Colonel, Colonel)

S. S. Batchelder (Major, Lieutenant Colonel)

Charles M. Bradford (Major)

Frederick H. Farrar, Jr. (Major, Lieutenant Colonel)

John A. Jacques (Major, Lieutenant Colonel, Colonel)

Frederick M. Kent (Major, Lieutenant Colonel)

James Strawbridge (Major, Lieutenant Colonel, Colonel)

Douglas West (Major)

Assignments: Pensacola, Florida (April-October 1861)

Army of Pensacola, Department of Alabama and West Florida (October 1861-February 1862)

D. W. Adams' Brigade, 2nd Corps, Second Grand Division, Army of the Mississippi, Department #2 (March 1862)

Gladden's-Gardner's Brigade, Withers' Division, 2nd Corps, Army of the Mississippi, Department #2 (March-June 1862)

Manigault's Brigade, Reserve Corps, Army of the Mississippi, Department #2 (June-July 1862)

Manigault's Brigade, Withers' Division, Army of the Mississippi, Department #2 (July-August 1862)

Manigault's Brigade, Withers' Division, Right Wing, Army of the Mississippi, Department #2 (August-November 1862)

Gardner's Brigade, Withers' Division, 1st Corps, Army of Tennessee (November 1862-January 1863)

Artillery Reserve, Army of Tennessee (July-August 1863)

Liddell's Brigade, Liddell's Division, Walker's Reserve Corps, Army of Tennessee (September 1863)

Liddell's Brigade, Cleburne's Division, 2nd Corps, Army of Tennessee (September-November 1863)

General Headquarters, Army of Tennessee (November 1863-February 1864)

Adams'-Gibson's, Brigade, Stewart's-Clayton's Division, 2nd Corps, Army of Tennessee (April 1864-February 1865)

Gibson's Brigade, District of the Gulf, Department of Alabama, Mississippi, and East Louisiana (February-April 1865)

Gibson's Brigade, Maury's Command, Department of Alabama, Mississippi, and East Louisiana (April-May 1865)

Battles: Santa Rosa Island [two companies] (October 8-9, 1861)

Pensacola (November 22-23, 1861)

Purdy Expedition and Crump's Landing operations [detachment] (March 9-14, 1862)
Yellow Creek [detachment] (March 14-15, 1862)
Shiloh (April 6-7, 1862)
Corinth Campaign (April-June 1862)
Kentucky Campaign (August 1862)
Murfreesboro (December 31, 1862-January 3, 1863)
Tullahoma Campaign (June-July 1863)
Chickamauga (September 19-20, 1863)
Chattanooga Siege (September-November 1863)
Chattanooga (November 23-25, 1863)
Atlanta Campaign (May-September 1864)
New Hope Church (May 25-June 4, 1864)
Atlanta (July 22, 1864)
Ezra Church (July 28, 1864)
Atlanta Siege (July-September 1864)
Jonesboro (August 31-September 1, 1864)
Nashville (December 15-16, 1864)
Mobile (March 17-April 12, 1865)
Spanish Fort (March 27-April 8, 1865)

132. LOUISIANA 2ND INFANTRY BATTALION

See: LOUISIANA 1ST SPECIAL INFANTRY BATTALION

133. LOUISIANA 2ND SPECIAL INFANTRY BATTALION

Organization: Organized with five companies probably at Camp Moore on June 14, 1861. One company was detached on July 22, 1861. Increased to a regiment and designated as the 10th Infantry Regiment on July 22, 1861.
First Commander: Felix Dumonteil (Major)
Assignment: Department #1 (June-July 1861)
Further Reading: Jones, Terry L., *Lee's Tigers: The Louisiana Infantry in the Army of Northern Virginia*. Buckley, Cornelius M., S.J., translator, *A Frenchman, a Chaplain, a Rebel: The War Letters of Pere Louis- Hippolyte Gache, S.J.*

134. LOUISIANA 2ND ZOUAVES INFANTRY BATTALION

Organization: Organized with two companies on April 22, 1862. Attached to Waul's (Texas) Legion by May 1863. Regiment surrendered at Vicksburg, Warren County, Mississippi on July 4, 1863. Paroled at Vicksburg, Warren County, Mississippi in July 1863. Reorganization attempted in late 1863. Broken up in January 1864.
First Commander: St. Leon Dupeire (Major)

Assignments: Department #1 (April-May 1862)
Vicksburg, Department #1 (May-June 1862)
Department of Southern Mississippi and East Louisiana (June-July 1862)
Smith's Brigade, District of the Mississippi, Department #2 (July 1862)
4th Sub-district, District of the Mississippi, Department #2 (July-August 1862)
Unattached, Lovell's Division, District of the Mississippi, Army of West Tennessee, Department #2 (September-October 1862)
Unattached, Lovell's Division, Army of West Tennessee, Department of Mississippi and East Louisiana (October 1862)
Waul's Legion, Loring's Division, Lovell's Corps, Army of North Mississippi, Department of Mississippi and East Louisiana (December 1862-January 1863)
Waul's Legion, Loring's Division, Army of the Department of Mississippi and East Louisiana (January 1863)
Waul's Legion, 2nd Military District, Department of Mississippi and East Louisiana (January-March 1863)
Moore's Brigade, Loring's Division, 2nd Military District, Department of Mississippi and East Louisiana (April 1863)
Moore's Brigade, Loring's Division, Department of Mississippi and East Louisiana (April 1863)
Waul's Legion, Stevenson's Division, Department of Mississippi and East Louisiana (April-July 1863)
Battles: New Orleans (April 18-25, 1862)
Vicksburg Bombardments (May 18-July 27, 1862)
Corinth (October 3-4, 1862)
Vicksburg Campaign (May-July 1863)
Vicksburg Siege (May-July 1863)
Bayou Portage (November 23, 1863)

135. LOUISIANA 2ND INFANTRY REGIMENT

Organization: Organized for 12 months at Camp Walker, New Orleans on May 11, 1861. Mustered into Confederate service for 12 months on May 11, 1861. Reorganized for the war on May 1, 1862. Surrendered at Appomattox Court House, Virginia on April 9, 1865.
First Commander: Lewis G. DeRussy (Colonel)
Field Officers: Richard W. Ashton (Major)
Ross E. Burke (Lieutenant Colonel, Colonel)
Michael A. Grogan (Major, Lieutenant Colonel)
William M. Levy (Captain, Colonel)
Isaiah T. Norwood (Major, Colonel)
Martin C. Redwine (Major)

Jesse M. William (Lieutenant Colonel, Colonel)
John S. Young (Lieutenant Colonel)
Assignments: Department of the Peninsula (May-October 1861)
McLaws' Brigade, Department of the Peninsula (October 1861)
McLaws' Division, Department of the Peninsula (January-April 1862)
H. Cobb's Brigade, McLaws' Division, Magruder's Command, Department of Northern Virginia (April-May 1862)
H. Cobb's Brigade, Magruder's Division, Army of Northern Virginia (May-June 1862)
H. Cobb's Brigade, Magruder's Division, Magruder's Command, Army of Northern Virginia (June-July 1862)
H. Cobb's Brigade, McLaws' Division, 1st Corps, Army of Northern Virginia (July 1862)
2nd Louisiana Brigade, McLaws' Division, 1st Corps, Army of Northern Virginia (July 1862)
2nd Louisiana Brigade, A. P. Hill's Division, 2nd Corps, Army of Northern Virginia (July 1862)
2nd Louisiana Brigade, Jackson's-Trimble's Division, 2nd Corps, Army of Northern Virginia (August 1862-May 1864)
Consolidated Louisiana Brigade, Early's-Gordon's Division, 2nd Corps, Army of Northern Virginia (May-June 1864)
Consolidated Louisiana Brigade, Gordon's Division, Valley District, Department of Northern Virginia (June-December 1864)
Consolidated Louisiana Brigade, Gordon's Division, 2nd Corps, Army of Northern Virginia (December 1864-April 1865)
Battles: Yorktown Siege (April-May 1862)
Lee's Mill (April 5, 1862)
Lee's Mill (April 16, 1862)
Seven Pines (May 31-June 1, 1862)
Seven Days Battles (June 25-July 1, 1862)
Malvern Hill (July 1, 1862)
Cedar Mountain (August 9, 1862)
2nd Bull Run (August 28-30, 1862)
Harpers Ferry (September 12-15, 1862)
Antietam (September 17, 1862)
Fredericksburg (December 13, 1862)
Chancellorsville (May 1-4, 1863)
2nd Winchester (June 14-15, 1863)
Gettysburg (July 1-3, 1863)
Bristoe Campaign (October 1863)
Mine Run Campaign (November-December 1863)

The Wilderness (May 5-6, 1864)
Spotsylvania Court House (May 8-21, 1864)
North Anna (May 23-26, 1864)
Cold Harbor (June 1-3, 1864)
Lynchburg Campaign (May-June 1864)
Monocacy (July 9, 1864)
Kernstown (July 24, 1864)
Shepherdstown (August 25, 1864)
3rd Winchester (September 19, 1864)
Fisher's Hill (September 22, 1864)
Cedar Creek (October 19, 1864)
Petersburg Siege [from December] (June 1864-April 1865)
Hatcher's Run (February 5-7, 1865)
Fort Stedman (March 25, 1865)
Petersburg Final Assault (April 2, 1865)
Sayler's Creek (April 6, 1865)
Appomattox Court House (April 9, 1865)
Further Reading: Jones, Terry L., *Lee's Tigers: The Louisiana Infantry in the Army of Northern Virginia.*

136. LOUISIANA 3RD INFANTRY BATTALION

Organization: Organized with eight companies for the war at Camp Pulaski, near Amite on June 16, 1861. Increased to a regiment and designated as the 15th Infantry Regiment on July 24, 1862.
First Commander: Charles M. Bradford (Lieutenant Colonel)
Field Officers: Edmund Pendleton (Major, Lieutenant Colonel)
McGavock Goodwyn (Major)
Robert A. Wilkinson (Major)
Assignments: Department of Norfolk (September 1861-March 1862)
J. R. Anderson's Brigade, Department of North Carolina (April 1862)
J. R. Anderson's Brigade, Department of Northern Virginia (April-May 1862)
J. R. Anderson's Brigade, A. P. Hill's Division, Army of Northern Virginia (May-June 1862)
J. R. Anderson's Brigade, A. P. Hill's Division, 1st Corps, Army of Northern Virginia (June-July 1862)
Battles: Seven Days Battles (June 25-July 1, 1862)
Beaver Dam Creek (June 26, 1862)
Frayser's Farm [not engaged] (June 30, 1862)
Further Reading: Jones, Terry L., *Lee's Tigers: The Louisiana Infantry in the Army of Northern Virginia.*

137. LOUISIANA 3RD INFANTRY REGIMENT

Organization: Organized with eight companies at Camp Walker, New Orleans on May 11, 1861. Later increased to 10 companies. Mustered into Confederate service on May 11, 1861. Regiment surrendered at Vicksburg, Warren County, Mississippi on July 4, 1863. Paroled at Vicksburg, Warren County, Mississippi in July 1863. Declared exchanged on September 12, 1863. Those members of the regiment east of the Mississippi River were consolidated with similar portions of the 17th, 21st (Smith's- Higgins'-Patton's), 22nd (Theard's-Herrick's), 26th, 27th, 29th and 31st Infantry Regiments and designated as the 22nd Consolidated Infantry Regiment at Enterprise, Mississippi on January 26, 1864. They became Company H, of that regiment. Balance of the regiment reorganized at Pineville, Louisiana in July 1864. Surrendered by General E. K. Smith, commanding Trans-Mississippi Department, on May 26, 1865.

First Commander: Louis Hébert (Colonel)

Field Officers: Frank C. Armstrong (Colonel)
Jerome B. Gilmore (Lieutenant Colonel, Colonel)
Samuel M. Hyams, Sr. (Lieutenant Colonel)
David Pierson (Major, Lieutenant Colonel)
John S. Richards (Major)
Samuel D. Russell (Major, Lieutenant Colonel, Colonel)
William F. Tunnard (Major)

Assignments: McCulloch's Brigade, Indian Territory (May-September 1861)
McCulloch's Division, Department #2 (September-December 1861)
Hébert's Brigade, McCulloch's Division, Department #2 (December 1861-January 1862)
Hébert's Brigade, McCulloch's Division, Trans-Mississippi District, Department #2 (January-March 1862)
Hébert's Brigade, Price's-Little's Division, Army of the West, Department #2 (March-October 1862)
Hébert's Brigade, Bowen's Division, Price's Corps, Army of West Tennessee, Department of Mississippi and East Louisiana (October 1862)
Hébert's Brigade, Maury's Division, Price's Corps, Army of West Tennessee, Department of Mississippi and East Louisiana (October-December 1862)
Hébert's Brigade, Maury's Division, Price's Corps, Army of North Mississippi, Department of Mississippi and East Louisiana (December 1862-January 1863)
Hébert's Brigade, Maury's-Forney's Division, 2nd Military District, Department of Mississippi and East Louisiana (January-April 1863)
Hébert's Brigade, Forney's Division, Department of Mississippi and East Louisiana (April-July 1863)

Thomas' Brigade, Mounton's Division, [at Alexandria], District of West Louisiana, Trans-Mississippi Department (November 1863)

Thomas' Brigade, Mouton's-Polignac's Division, District of West Louisiana, Trans-Mississippi Department (July-September 1864)

1st (Thomas') Louisiana Brigade, 2nd (Polignac's) Division, 1st Corps, Trans-Mississippi Department (September 1864-May 1865)

Battles: Wilson's Creek (August 10, 1861)

Pea Ridge (March 7-8, 1862)

Corinth Campaign (April-June 1862)

Farmington (May 9, 1862)

Iuka (September 19, 1862)

Corinth (October 3-4, 1862)

vs. Greenville Expedition (April 2-14, 1863)

Haynes' and Snyder's Bluffs (April 29-May 1, 1863)

Vicksburg Campaign (May-July 1863)

Vicksburg Siege (May-July 1863)

Further Reading: Tunnard, William F., *A Southern Record: The History of the Third Regiment Louisiana Infantry*. Watson, William, *Life in the Confederate Army*.

138. LOUISIANA 4TH INFANTRY BATTALION

Organization: Organized with six companies for the war at Richmond, Virginia on July 10, 1861. Field consolidation with the 25th Infantry Regiment from February to April 1865. Consolidated with the 19th, 20th, and 25th Infantry Regiments and designated as Companies F and G, Pelican Consolidated Infantry Regiment in April 1865.

First Commander: George C. Waddill (Major)

Field Officers: Samuel L. Bishop (Major)

Duncan Buie (Major)

John McEnery (Major, Lieutenant Colonel)

Assignments: Army of the Kanawha (October-December 1861)

Department of South Carolina and Georgia (December 1861-April 1862)

Smith's Brigade, Military District of Georgia, Department of South Carolina, Georgia, and Florida (April-June 1862)

2nd Military District of South Carolina, Department of South Carolina, Georgia, and Florida (June 1862)

Military District of Georgia, Department of South Carolina, Georgia, and Florida (June 1862-January 1863)

Harrison's Brigade, District of the Cape Fear, Department of North Carolina (January-February 1863)

Taliaferro's Brigade, Military District of Georgia, Department of South Carolina, Georgia, and Florida (February-April 1863)
Walker's Brigade, Department of the West (May-June 1863)
Wilson's Brigade, Walker's Division, Department of the West (June-July 1863)
Wilson's Brigade, Walker's Division, Department of Mississippi and East Louisiana (July-August 1863)
Wilson's Brigade, Walker's Division, Walker's Reserve Corps, Army of Tennessee (September 1863)
Wilson's Brigade, Walker's Division, Longstreet's Corps, Army of Tennessee (September-November 1863)
D. W. Adams'-Gibson's Brigade, Stewart's-Clayton's Division, 2nd Corps, Army of Tennessee (November 1863-January 1865)
Gibson's Brigade, District of the Gulf, Department of Alabama, Mississippi, and East Louisiana (March-April 1865)
Battles: Cotton Hill [skirmishes] (October 31-November 12, 1861)
Secessionville (June 16, 1862)
Vicksburg Campaign (May-July 1863)
Jackson (May 14, 1863)
Jackson Siege (July 10-17, 1863)
Chickamauga (September 19-20, 1863)
Chattanooga Siege (September-November 1863)
Chattanooga (November 23-25, 1863)
Atlanta Campaign (May-September 1864)
Resaca (May 14-15, 1864)
New Hope Church (May 25-June 4, 1864)
Atlanta (July 22, 1864)
Ezra Church (July 28, 1864)
Atlanta Siege (July-September 1864)
Jonesboro (August 31-September 1, 1864)
Mobile (March 17-April 12, 1865)
Spanish Fort (March 27-April 8, 1865)

139. LOUISIANA 4TH INFANTRY REGIMENT

Organization: Organized at Camp Moore on May 25, 1861. Mustered into Confederate service for 12 months at Camp Moore on May 25, 1861. Detachment surrendered at Port Hudson on July 9, 1863. Field consolidation with the 30th Infantry Battalion from November 1864 to March 1865. Field consolidation with the 13th Infantry Regiment, 30th Infantry Battalion, and 14th Sharpshooters Battalion from February to May 4, 1865. Surrendered by Lieutenant Richard Taylor, commanding the Department of Alabama, Mississippi, and East Louisiana, at Citronelle, Alabama on May 4, 1865.

First Commander: Robert J. Barrow (Colonel)
Field Officers: Henry W. Allen (Lieutenant Colonel, Colonel)
Samuel E. Hunter (Major, Lieutenant Colonel, Colonel)
William F. Pennington (Major, Lieutenant Colonel)
E. J. Pullen (Major)
Thomas E. Vick (Major)
Assignments: Department #1 (May 1861-February 1862)
Mouton's Brigade, 1st Corps, 2nd Grand Division, Army of the Mississippi, Department #2 (March 1862)
Gibson's Brigade, Ruggles' Division, 2nd Corps, Army of the Mississippi, Department #2 (March-April 1862)
Anderson's Brigade, Ruggles' Division, 2nd Corps, Army of the Mississippi, Department #2 (April-May 1862)
2nd Sub-district, District of the Mississippi, Department #2 (July-August 1862)
Allen's Brigade, Ruggles' Division, Breckinridge's Command, District of the Mississippi, Department #2 (August 1862)
1st Sub-district, District of the Mississippi, Department #2 (August-October 1862)
Department of Mississippi and East Louisiana (October 1862)
3rd Military District, District of East Louisiana, Department of Mississippi and East Louisiana (October 1862-January 1863)
Maxey's Brigade, District of East Louisiana, Department of Mississippi and East Louisiana (January-May 1863)
Miles' Brigade, District of East Louisiana, Department of Mississippi and East Louisiana [detachment] (May-July 1863)
Maxey's Brigade, Loring's Division, Department of the West (May-June 1863)
Maxey's Brigade, French's Division, Department of the West (June-July 1863)
Maxey's Brigade, French's Division, Department of Mississippi and East Louisiana (July-August 1863)
Cantey's Brigade, Department of the Gulf (September-December 1863)
Quarles' Brigade, Breckinridge's Division, 2nd Corps, Army of Tennessee (December 1863-February 1864)
Quarles' Brigade, Department of the Gulf (February-April 1864)
Quarles' Brigade, District of the Gulf, Department of Alabama, Mississippi, and East Louisiana (April-May 1864)
Quarles' Brigade, Walthall's Division, Army of Mississippi (June-July 1864)
Gibson's Brigade, Stewart's-Clayton's Division, 2nd Corps, Army of Tennessee (July 1864-January 1865)
Gibson's Brigade, District of the Gulf, Department of Alabama, Mississippi, and East Louisiana (March-April 1865)

Gibson's Brigade, Department of Alabama, Mississippi, and East Louisiana (April-May 1865)
Battles: Shiloh (April 6-7, 1862)
Vicksburg Bombardments (May 18-July 27, 1862)
Baton Rouge (August 5, 1862)
Port Hudson *vs.* USS *Essex's* crews [detachment] (August 15, 1862)
vs. USS *Indianola* (February 24, 1863)
Grierson's Raid (April 17-May 2, 1863)
Port Hudson Siege [detachment] (May-July 1863)
Jackson Siege (July 10-17, 1863)
Atlanta Campaign (May-September 1864)
New Hope Church (May 25-June 4, 1864)
Peach Tree Creek (July 20, 1864)
Atlanta (July 22, 1864)
Ezra Church (July 28, 1864)
Atlanta Siege (July-September 1864)
Jonesboro (August 31-September 1, 1864)
Franklin [in reserve] (November 30, 1864)
Nashville (December 15-16, 1864)
Mobile (March 17-April 12, 1865)
Spanish Fort (March 27-April 8, 1865)
Further Reading: Lambert, Samuel, *A Record of the Late Fourth Louisiana Reg't., C.S.A.* Richards, A. P., *The Saint Helena Rifles.*

140. LOUISIANA 5TH INFANTRY BATTALION

Organization: Organized with six companies for the war at Columbus, Kentucky in August 1861. Increased to a regiment and designated as the 21st (Kennedy's) Infantry Regiment February 9, 1862.
First Commander: John B. G. Kennedy (Lieutenant Colonel)
Field Officer: John Newman (Major)
Assignments: Columbus, Kentucky, Department #2 (August-September 1861)
Marks' Brigade, McCown's Division, 1st Geographical Division, Department #2 (September 1861-February 1862)
Marks' Brigade, McCown's Command, 1st Geographical Division, Department #2 (February 1862)
Battle: Belmont (November 7, 1861)

141. LOUISIANA 5TH INFANTRY REGIMENT

Organization: Organized at Camp Moore on May 25, 1861. Mustered into Confederate service at Camp Moore on May 25, 1861. Mustered into Confed-

erate service for the war at Camp Moore on June 4, 1861. Field consolidation with the 6th and 7th Infantry Regiments from November 1864 to April 9, 1865. Surrendered at Appomattox Court House, Virginia on April 9, 1865.
First Commander: Theodore G. Hunt (Colonel)
Field Officers: William T. Dean (Major)
Henry Forno (Lieutenant Colonel, Colonel)
Alexander Hart (Major)
Bruce Menger (Lieutenant Colonel)
Assignments: Department of the Peninsula (June-October 1861)
Hunt's Brigade, Department of the Peninsula (October 1861)
McLaws' Division, Department of the Peninsula (January-April 1862)
McLaws' Brigade, McLaws' Division, Magruder's Command, Department of Northern Virginia (April-May 1862)
McLaws' Brigade, Magruder's Division, Army of Northern Virginia (May-June 1862)
Semmes' Brigade, McLaws' Division, Magruder's Command, Army of Northern Virginia (June-July 1862)
Semmes' Brigade, McLaws' Division, 1st Corps, Army of Northern Virginia (July 1862)
1st Louisiana Brigade, Ewell's-Early's Division, 2nd Corps, Army of Northern Virginia (July 1862-May 1864)
Consolidated Louisiana Brigade, Early's-Gordon's Division, 2nd Corps, Army of Northern Virginia (May-June 1864)
Consolidated Louisiana Brigade, Gordon's Division, Valley District, Department of Northern Virginia (June-December 1864)
Consolidated Louisiana Brigade, Gordon's Division, 2nd Corps, Army of Northern Virginia (December 1864-April 1865)
Battles: Yorktown Siege (April-May 1862)
Lee's Mill (April 16, 1862)
Williamsburg [skirmish] (May 4, 1862)
New Bridge (May 24, 1862)
Seven Days Battles (June 25-July 1, 1862)
Savage's Station (June 29, 1862)
White Oak Swamp (June 29, 1862)
Malvern Hill (July 1, 1862)
Cedar Mountain (August 9, 1862)
Bristoe Station (August 26, 1862)
Kettle Run (August 27, 1862)
2nd Bull Run (August 28-30, 1862)
Chantilly (September 1, 1862)
Harpers Ferry (September 12-15, 1862)

Antietam (September 17, 1862)
Fredericksburg (December 13, 1862)
Rappahannock River, near Fredericksburg (April 29, 1863)
Chancellorsville (May 1-4, 1863)
Salem Church (May 4, 1863)
2nd Winchester (June 14-15, 1863)
Gettysburg (July 1-3, 1863)
Raccoon Ford [one company] (September 17, 1863)
Bristoe Campaign (October 1863)
Rappahannock Station (November 7, 1863)
Mine Run Campaign (November-December 1863)
The Wilderness (May 5-6, 1864)
Spotsylvania Court House (May 8-21, 1864)
North Anna (May 23-26, 1864)
Cold Harbor (June 1-3, 1864)
Lynchburg Campaign (May-June 1864)
Monocacy (July 9, 1864)
Kernstown (July 24, 1864)
Shepherdstown (August 25, 1864)
3rd Winchester (September 19, 1864)
Fisher's Hill (September 22, 1864)
Cedar Creek (October 19, 1864)
Petersburg Siege [from December] (June 1864-April 1865)
Hatcher's Run (February 5-7, 1865)
Fort Stedman (March 25, 1865)
Petersburg Final Assault (April 2, 1865)
Sayler's Creek (April 6, 1865)
Appomattox Court House (April 9, 1865)

Further Reading: Jones, Terry L., *Lee's Tigers: The Louisiana Infantry in the Army of Northern Virginia.*

142. LOUISIANA 6TH (MORRISON'S) INFANTRY BATTALION

Organization: Organized on May 14, 1862. Increased to a regiment and designated as the 31st Infantry Regiment on June 11, 1862. This unit does not appear separately in the *Official Records*.

First Commander: Charles H. Morrison (Lieutenant Colonel)

Field Officer: Sidney H. Griffin (Major)

Assignment: Department #1 (May-June 1862)

143. LOUISIANA 6TH (REICHARD'S) INFANTRY BATTALION

Nickname: Lovell Battalion

Organization: Organized with four companies at Camp Lewis, New Orleans in September 1861. Increased to a regiment and designated as the 20th Infantry Regiment on January 3, 1862. This unit does not appear separately in the *Official Records*.
First Commander: Augustus Reichard (Major)
Assignment: Department #1 (September 1861-January 1862)

144. LOUISIANA 6TH INFANTRY REGIMENT

Nickname: Irish Brigade
Organization: Organized at Camp Moore on May 23, 1861. Mustered into Confederate service with eight companies for the war and two for 12 months on June 4, 1861. Reorganized in May 1862. Field consolidation with the 5th and 7th Infantry Regiments from November 1864 to April 9, 1865. Surrendered at Appomattox Court House, Virginia on April 9, 1865.
First Commander: Isaac G. Seymour (Colonel)
Field Officers: George W. Christy (Major)
Joseph Hanlon (Lieutenant Colonel)
Samuel L. Jones (Major)
Louis Lay (Lieutenant Colonel)
Arthur McArthur, Jr. (Major)
William H. Manning (Major)
William Monaghan (Lieutenant Colonel, Colonel)
Nathaniel G. Offutt (Major, Lieutenant Colonel, Colonel)
Henry B. Strong (Lieutenant Colonel, Colonel)
Assignments: Alexandria Line (June 1861)
Ewell's Brigade, Army of the Potomac (June-July 1861)
Ewell's Brigade, 1st Corps, Army of the Potomac (July 1861)
W. H. T. Walker's-Taylor's Brigade, 1st Corps, Army of the Potomac (July-October 1861)
1st Louisiana Brigade, 1st Corps, Potomac District, Department of Northern Virginia (October-November 1861)
1st Louisiana Brigade, E. K. Smith's Division, 1st Corps, Army of Northern Virginia (November 1861-February 1862)
1st Louisiana Brigade, E. K. Smith's-Ewell's Division, Department of Northern Virginia (February-May 1862)
1st Louisiana Brigade, Ewell's Division, Valley District, Department of Northern Virginia (May-June 1862)
1st Louisiana Brigade, Ewell's-Early's Division, 2nd Corps, Army of Northern Virginia (June 1862-May 1864)
Consolidated Louisiana Brigade, Early's-Gordon's Division, 2nd Corps, Army of Northern Virginia (May-June 1864)

Consolidated Louisiana Brigade, Gordon's Division, Valley District, Department of Northern Virginia (June-December 1864)
Consolidated Louisiana Brigade, Gordon's Division, 2nd Corps, Army of Northern Virginia (December 1864-April 1865)

Battles: 1st Bull Run (July 21, 1861)
Shenandoah Valley Campaign (May-June 1862)
Front Royal [in reserve] (May 23, 1862)
Middletown (May 24, 1862)
1st Winchester (May 25, 1862)
Mount Carmel (June 1, 1862)
Cross Keys (June 8-9, 1862)
Port Republic (June 9, 1862)
Seven Days Battles (June 25-July 1, 1862)
Hundley's Corner (June 26, 1862)
Gaines' Mill (June 27, 1862)
Malvern Hill (July 1, 1862)
Cedar Mountain (August 9, 1862)
Bristoe Station (August 26, 1862)
Kettle Run (August 27, 1862)
2nd Bull Run (August 28-30, 1862)
Chantilly (September 1, 1862)
Antietam (September 17, 1862)
Fredericksburg (December 13, 1862)
Rappahannock River, near Fredericksburg (April 29, 1863)
Chancellorsville (May 1-4, 1863)
Marye's Heights (May 3, 1863)
Salem Church (May 4, 1863)
2nd Winchester (June 14-15, 1863)
Gettysburg (July 1-3, 1863)
Bristoe Campaign (October 1863)
Rappahannock Station (November 7, 1863)
Mine Run Campaign (November-December 1863)
The Wilderness (May 5-6, 1864)
Spotsylvania Court House (May 8-21, 1864)
North Anna (May 23-26, 1864)
Cold Harbor (June 1-3, 1864)
Lynchburg Campaign (May-June 1864)
Monocacy (July 9, 1864)
3rd Winchester (September 19, 1864)
Fisher's Hill (September 22, 1864)
Cedar Creek (October 19, 1864)

Petersburg Siege [from December] (June 1864-April 1865)
Hatcher's Run (February 5-7, 1865)
Fort Stedman (March 25, 1865)
Sayler's Creek (April 6, 1865)
Appomattox Court House (April 9, 1865)
Further Reading: Jones, Terry L., *Lee's Tigers: The Louisiana Infantry in the Army of Northern Virginia.*

145. LOUISIANA 7TH INFANTRY BATTALION

Also Known As: 19th Infantry Battalion
Nicknames: St. Paul's Foot Rifles,, 3
Organization: Organized with two companies at Manassas on October 1, 1861. The third company was assigned on November 1, 1861. Served attached to the Washington Artillery Battalion as sharpshooters. Attached to the 1st Special Infantry Battalion on May 31, 1862. Companies B and C were assigned to the 3rd Louisiana Infantry Battalion and designated as the 15th Infantry Regiment on July 27, 1862. Many of the battalion's members were asigned to the Washington Artillery Battalion in the summer of 1862.
First Commander: Henri St. Paul (Major)
Field Officer: McGavock Goodwyn (Major [acting])
Assignments: Reserve Artillery, Potomac District, Department of Northern Virginia (January-March 1862)
Reserve Artillery, Department of Northern Virginia (March-May 1862)
R. H. Anderson's Brigade, Longstreet's Division, Army of Northern Virginia (May-June 1862)
Taylor's Brigade, Ewell's Division, 2nd Corps, Army of Northern Virginia (June 1862)
Battles: Yorktown Siege (April-May 1862)
Williamsburg (May 5, 1862)
Seven Pines (May 31-June 1, 1862)
Seven Days Battles (June 25-July 1, 1862)
Gaines' Mill (June 27, 1862)
Further Reading: Jones, Terry L., *Lee's Tigers: The Louisiana Infantry in the Army of Northern Virginia.*

146. LOUISIANA 7TH INFANTRY REGIMENT

Nickname: Pelican Regiment
Organization: Organized at Camp Moore in May 1861. Mustered into Confederate service for the war at Camp Moore on June 5, 1861. Field consolidation with the 5th and 6th Infantry Regiments from November 1864 to April 9, 1865. Surrendered at Appomattox Court House, Virginia on April 9, 1865.

First Commander: Harry T. Hays (Colonel)
Field Officers: Charles DeChoisel (Lieutenant Colonel)
David B. Penn (Major, Lieutenant Colonel, Colonel)
Thomas M. Terry (Major, Lieutenant Colonel)
J. Moore (Major)
Assignments: Early's Brigade, Army of the Potomac (June-July 1861)
Early's Brigade, 1st Corps, Army of the Potomac (July 1861)
W. H. T. Walker's-Taylor's Brigade, 1st Corps, Army of the Potomac (July-October 1861)
1st Louisiana Brigade, 1st Corps, Potomac District, Department of Northern Virginia (October-November 1861)
1st Louisiana Brigade, E. K. Smith's Division, 1st Corps, Army of Northern Virginia (November 1861-February 1862)
1st Louisiana Brigade, E. K. Smith's-Ewell's Division, Department of Northern Virginia (February-May 1862)
1st Louisiana Brigade, Ewell's Division, Valley District, Department of Northern Virginia (May-June 1862)
1st Louisiana Brigade, Ewell's-Early's Division, 2nd Corps, Army of Northern Virginia (June 1862-May 1864)
Consolidated Louisiana Brigade, Early's-Gordon's Division, 2nd Corps, Army of Northern Virginia (May-June 1864)
Consolidated Louisiana Brigade, Gordon's Division, Valley District, Department of Northern Virginia (June-December 1864)
Consolidated Louisiana Brigade, Gordon's Division, 2nd Corps, Army of Northern Virginia (December 1864-April 1865)
Battles: Blackburn's Ford (July 18, 1861)
1st Bull Run (July 21, 1861)
Shenandoah Valley Campaign (May-June 1862)
Somerville Heights [skirmish] [detachment] (May 7, 1862)
Front Royal [in reserve] (May 23, 1862)
Middletown (May 24, 1862)
1st Winchester (May 25, 1862)
Mount Carmel (June 1, 1862)
Cross Keys (June 8-9, 1862)
Port Republic (June 9, 1862)
Seven Days Battles (June 25-July 1, 1862)
Gaines' Mill (June 27, 1862)
Malvern Hill (July 1, 1862)
Cedar Mountain (August 9, 1862)
Bristoe Station (August 26, 1862)
Kettle Run (August 27, 1862)

2nd Bull Run (August 28-30, 1862)
Chantilly (September 1, 1862)
Harpers Ferry (September 12-15, 1862)
Antietam (September 17, 1862)
Fredericksburg (December 13, 1862)
Chancellorsville (May 1-4, 1863)
Marye's Heights (May 3, 1863)
2nd Winchester (June 14-15, 1863)
Gettysburg (July 1-3, 1863)
Bristoe Campaign (October 1863)
Rappahannock Station (November 7, 1863)
Mine Run Campaign (November-December 1863)
The Wilderness (May 5-6, 1864)
Spotsylvania Court House (May 8-21, 1864)
North Anna (May 23-26, 1864)
Cold Harbor (June 1-3, 1864)
Lynchburg Campaign (May-June 1864)
Monocacy (July 9, 1864)
Kernstown (July 24, 1864)
Shepherdstown (August 25, 1864)
3rd Winchester (September 19, 1864)
Fisher's Hill (September 22, 1864)
Cedar Creek (October 19, 1864)
Petersburg Siege [from December] (June 1864-April 1865)
Hatcher's Run (February 5-7, 1865)
Fort Stedman (March 25, 1865)
Petersburg Final Assault (April 2, 1865)
Sayler's Creek (April 6, 1865)
Appomattox Court House (April 9, 1865)
Further Reading: Jones, Terry L., *Lee's Tigers: The Louisiana Infantry in the Army of Northern Virginia.*

147. LOUISIANA 8TH INFANTRY BATTALION

Nickname: Pinkney Battalion
Organization: Organized with six companies at New Orleans in February 1862. Reduced to three companies and designated as the 8th Heavy Artillery Battalion at Vicksburg, Mississippi on May 5, 1862.
First Commander: William E. Pinkney (Lieutenant Colonel)
Field Officer: Fred N. Ogden (Major)
Assignment: Department #1 (February-May 1862)
Battle: New Orleans (April 18-25, 1862)

148. LOUISIANA 8TH INFANTRY REGIMENT

Organization: Organized at Camp Moore on June 15, 1861. Mustered into Confederate service with seven companies for the war and three companies for 12 months at Camp Moore on June 15, 1861. Reorganized for the war in April 1862. Surrendered at Appomattox Court House, Virginia on April 9, 1865.

First Commander: Henry B. Kelly (Colonel)

Field Officers: Alcibiades DeBlanc (Major, Lieutenant Colonel, Colonel)
German A. Lester (Major, Lieutenant Colonel)
Trevanion D. Lewis (Major, Lieutenant Colonel, Colonel)
Francis T. Nicholls (Lieutenant Colonel)
John B. E. Prados (Major)

Assignments: Unattached, 1st Corps, Army of the Potomac (July 1861)
W. H. T. Walker's-Taylor's Brigade, 1st Corps, Army of the Potomac (July-October 1861)
1st Louisiana Brigade, 1st Corps, Potomac District, Department of Northern Virginia (October-November 1861)
1st Louisiana Brigade, E. K. Smith's Division, 1st Corps, Army of Northern Virginia (November 1861-February 1862)
1st Louisiana Brigade, E. K. Smith's-Ewell's Division, Department of Northern Virginia (February-May 1862)
1st Louisiana Brigade, Ewell's Division, Valley District, Department of Northern Virginia (May-June 1862)
1st Louisiana Brigade, Ewell's-Early's Division, 2nd Corps, Army of Northern Virginia (June 1862-May 1864)
Consolidated Louisiana Brigade, Early's-Gordon's Division, 2nd Corps, Army of Northern Virginia (May-June 1864)
Consolidated Louisiana Brigade, Gordon's Division, Valley District, Department of Northern Virginia (June-December 1864)
Consolidated Louisiana Brigade, Gordon's Division, 2nd Corps, Army of Northern Virginia (December 1864-April 1865)

Battles: Secessionville (June 16, 1862)
1st Bull Run [not engaged] (July 21, 1861)
Shenandoah Valley Campaign (May-June 1862)
Front Royal (May 23, 1862)
Middletown (May 24, 1862)
1st Winchester (May 25, 1862)
Front Royal (May 30, 1862)
Mount Carmel (June 1, 1862)
Cross Keys (June 8-9, 1862)
Port Republic (June 9, 1862)
Seven Days Battles (June 25-July 1, 1862)

Gaines' Mill (June 27, 1862)
Malvern Hill (July 1, 1862)
Cedar Mountain (August 9, 1862)
Bristoe Station (August 26, 1862)
Kettle Run (August 27, 1862)
2nd Bull Run (August 28-30, 1862)
Chantilly (September 1, 1862)
Harpers Ferry (September 12-15, 1862)
Antietam (September 17, 1862)
Fredericksburg (December 13, 1862)
Chancellorsville (May 1-4, 1863)
Marye's Heights (May 3, 1863)
Salem Church (May 4, 1863)
2nd Winchester (June 14-15, 1863)
Gettysburg (July 1-3, 1863)
Bristoe Campaign (October 1863)
Rappahannock Station (November 7, 1863)
Mine Run Campaign (November-December 1863)
The Wilderness (May 5-6, 1864)
Spotsylvania Court House (May 8-21, 1864)
North Anna (May 23-26, 1864)
Cold Harbor (June 1-3, 1864)
Lynchburg Campaign (May-June 1864)
Monocacy (July 9, 1864)
3rd Winchester (September 19, 1864)
Fisher's Hill (September 22, 1864)
Cedar Creek (October 19, 1864)
Petersburg Siege [detachment] (June 1864-April 1865)
Fort Stedman (March 25, 1865)
Sayler's Creek (April 6, 1865)
Appomattox Court House (April 9, 1865)
Further Reading: Jones, Terry L., *Lee's Tigers: The Louisiana Infantry in the Army of Northern Virginia.*

149. LOUISIANA 9TH INFANTRY BATTALION

Also Known As: Louisiana 17th Infantry Battalion
Organization: Organized with three infantry and one cavalry company from Stewart's Legion at Camp Moore on May 15, 1862. Company D was assigned July 1862. Surrendered at Port Hudson, Louisiana on July 8, 1863. Paroled in July 1863. Company A was mounted in May 1864 and was subsequently

assigned to Gober's Mounted Infantry Regiment. The battalion itself was never reorganized following its exchange.
First Commander: Samuel Boyd (Lieutenant Colonel [temporary])
Field Officers: Thomas Bynum (Major)
Bolling F. Chinn (Major)
Assignments: Department of Southern Mississippi and East Louisiana (June-July 1862)
3rd Sub-district, District of the Mississippi, Department #2 (July 1862)
1st Sub-district, District of the Mississippi, Department #2 [detachment] (July 1862)
Allen's Brigade, Ruggles' Division, Breckinridge's Command, District of the Mississippi, Department #2 (July-August 1862)
1st Sub-district, District of the Mississippi, Department #2 (August-October 1862)
Department of Southern Mississippi and East Louisiana (October 1862)
Gregg's Brigade, 3rd Military District, Department of Mississippi and East Louisiana (October 1862-April 1863)
Miles' Brigade, 3rd Military District, Department of Mississippi and East Louisiana (April 1863-July 1864)
District of Southwest Mississippi and East Louisiana, Department of Alabama, Mississippi, and East Louisiana [Company A; mounted] (May-July 1864)
Battles: Baton Rouge (August 5, 1862)
Vicksburg Campaign (May-July 1863)
Vicksburg Siege (May-July 1863)

150. LOUISIANA 9TH INFANTRY REGIMENT

Organization: Organized at Camp Moore on July 6, 1861. Mustered into Confederate service with six companies for the war and four companies for 12 months on July 6, 1861. Reorganized on April 24, 1862. Surrendered at Appomattox Court House, Virginia on April 9, 1865.
First Commander: Richard Taylor (Colonel)
Field Officers: John J. Hodges (Major, Lieutenant Colonel)
James R. Kavanaugh (Major)
William R. Peck (Colonel)
Edward G. Randolph (Lieutenant Colonel, Colonel)
Alfred A. Singletary (Major)
Leroy A. Stafford (Colonel)
Nathaniel J. Walker (Major, Lieutenant Colonel)
Henry L. N. Williams (Major)
Assignments: Unattached, 1st Corps, Army of the Potomac (July 1861)

W. H. T. Walker's-Taylor's Brigade, 1st Corps, Army of the Potomac (July-October 1861)
1st Louisiana Brigade, 1st Corps, Potomac District, Department of Northern Virginia (October-November 1861)
1st Louisiana Brigade, E. K. Smith's Division, 1st Corps, Army of Northern Virginia (November 1861-February 1862)
1st Louisiana Brigade, E. K. Smith's-Ewell's Division, Department of Northern Virginia (February-May 1862)
1st Louisiana Brigade, Ewell's Division, Valley District, Department of Northern Virginia (May-June 1862)
1st Louisiana Brigade, Ewell's-Early's Division, 2nd Corps, Army of Northern Virginia (June 1862-May 1864)
Consolidated Louisiana Brigade, Early's-Gordon's Division, 2nd Corps, Army of Northern Virginia (May-June 1864)
Consolidated Louisiana Brigade, Gordon's Division, Valley District, Department of Northern Virginia (June-December 1864)
Consolidated Louisiana Brigade, Gordon's Division, 2nd Corps, Army of Northern Virginia (December 1864-April 1865)
Battles: Shenandoah Valley Campaign (May-June 1862)
Somerville Heights [skirmish] [one company] (May 7, 1862)
Front Royal [Company A] (May 23, 1862)
Middletown (May 24, 1862)
1st Winchester (May 25, 1862)
Front Royal (May 30, 1862)
Mount Carmel (June 1, 1862)
Cross Keys (June 8-9, 1862)
Port Republic (June 9, 1862)
Seven Days Battles (June 25-July 1, 1862)
Gaines' Mill (June 27, 1862)
Malvern Hill (July 1, 1862)
Cedar Mountain (August 9, 1862)
Bristoe Station (August 26, 1862)
2nd Bull Run (August 28-30, 1862)
Chantilly (September 1, 1862)
Harpers Ferry (September 12-15, 1862)
Antietam (September 17, 1862)
Fredericksburg (December 13, 1862)
Chancellorsville (May 1-4, 1863)
Marye's Heights (May 3, 1863)
Salem Church (May 4, 1863)
2nd Winchester (June 14-15, 1863)

Gettysburg (July 1-3, 1863)
Raccoon Ford [one company] (September 17, 1863)
Bristoe Campaign (October 1863)
Rappahannock Station (November 7, 1863)
Mine Run Campaign (November-December 1863)
The Wilderness (May 5-6, 1864)
Spotsylvania Court House (May 8-21, 1864)
North Anna (May 23-26, 1864)
Cold Harbor (June 1-3, 1864)
Lynchburg Campaign (May-June 1864)
Monocacy (July 9, 1864)
Kernstown (July 24, 1864)
Shepherdstown (August 25, 1864)
3rd Winchester (September 19, 1864)
Fisher's Hill (September 22, 1864)
Cedar Creek (October 19, 1864)
Petersburg Siege [detachment] (June 1864-April 1865)
Hatcher's Run (February 5-7, 1865)
Fort Stedman (March 25, 1865)
Petersburg Final Assault (April 2, 1865)
Sayler's Creek (April 6, 1865)
Appomattox Court House (April 9, 1865)
Further Reading: Jones, Terry L., *Lee's Tigers: The Louisiana Infantry in the Army of Northern Virginia.* Handerson, Henry E., *Yankee in Gray: The Civil War Memoirs of Henry E. Handerson with a Selection From His Wartime Letters.*

151. LOUISIANA 10TH INFANTRY BATTALION

Nickname: Yellow Jacket Battalion
Organization: Organized with six companies at St. Martinville on April 7, 1862. Consolidated with the Confederate (Louisiana) Guards Response Infantry Battalion and designated as the 33rd Infantry Regiment ca. October 10, 1862. This regiment was broken up and the battalions reorganized at Camp Bisland on November 22, 1862. Consolidated into four companies and consolidated with the 18th Infantry Regiment and designated as the 18th Consolidated Infantry Regiment at Simmesport on November 14, 1863.
First Commander: Valsin A. Fournet (Lieutenant Colonel)
Field Officers: Desire Beraud (Major)
Gabriel A. Fournet (Major, Lieutenant Colonel)
Arthur F. Simon (Major)
Assignments: Department #1 (April-May 1862)

District of West Louisiana and Texas, Trans-Mississippi Department (May-August 1862)
District of West Louisiana, Trans-Mississippi Department (August-October 1862)
Mouton's Brigade, District of West Louisiana, Trans-Mississippi Department (November 1862-November 1863)
Gray's Brigade, Mouton's-Polignac's Division, District of West Louisiana, Trans-Mississippi Department (November 1863)
Battles: Fort Bisland (April 13-14, 1863)
Red River Campaign (May 10-22, 1864)
Mansfield (April 8, 1864)
Pleasant Hill (April 9, 1864)

152. LOUISIANA 10TH INFANTRY REGIMENT

Organization: Organized by the addition of five companies to the 2nd Special Infantry Battalion at Camp Moore on July 22, 1861. Mustered into Confederate service for the war at Camp Moore on July 22, 1861. Field consolidation with the 15th Infantry Regiment from November 1864 to April 9, 1865. Surrendered at Appomattox Court House, Virginia on April 9, 1865.
First Commander: Antoine J. De Marigny (Colonel)
Field Officers: Jules C. Denis (Lieutenant Colonel)
Felix Dumonteil (Major)
John M. Leggett (Major, Lieutenant Colonel)
Henry D. Monier (Major, Lieutenant Colonel, Colonel)
William H. Spencer (Major, Lieutenant Colonel)
Eugene Waggaman (Lieutenant Colonel, Colonel)
Assignments: Department of the Peninsula (August-October 1861)
Sulakowski's Brigade, Department of the Peninsula (October 1861)
McLaws' Division, Department of the Peninsula (January-April 1862)
McLaws' Brigade, McLaws' Division, Magruder's Command, Department of Northern Virginia (April-May 1862)
McLaws' Brigade, Magruder's Division, Army of Northern Virginia (May-June 1862)
Semmes' Brigade, McLaws' Division, Magruder's Command, Army of Northern Virginia (June-July 1862)
Semmes' Brigade, McLaws' Division, 1st Corps, Army of Northern Virginia (July 1862)
2nd Louisiana Brigade, McLaws' Division, 1st Corps, Army of Northern Virginia (July 1862)
2nd Louisiana Brigade, A. P. Hill's Division, 2nd Corps, Army of Northern Virginia (July 1862)

2nd Louisiana Brigade, Jackson's-Johnson's Division, 2nd Corps, Army of Northern Virginia (August 1862-May 1864)
Consolidated Louisiana Brigade, Early's-Gordon's Division, 2nd Corps, Army of Northern Virginia (May-June 1864)
Consolidated Louisiana Brigade, Gordon's Division, Valley District, Department of Northern Virginia (June-December 1864)
Consolidated Louisiana Brigade, Gordon's Division, 2nd Corps, Army of Northern Virginia (December 1864-April 1865)
Battles: Yorktown Siege (April-May 1862)
Lee's Mills (April 5, 1862)
Lee's Mills (April 16, 1862)
Williamsburg [skirmish] (May 4, 1862)
Seven Days Battles (June 25-July 1, 1862)
Savage's Station (June 29, 1862)
Malvern Hill (July 1, 1862)
Allen's Farm (June 29, 1862)
Cedar Mountain (August 9, 1862)
Bristoe Station (August 26, 1862)
2nd Bull Run (August 28-30, 1862)
Chantilly (September 1, 1862)
Harpers Ferry (September 12-15, 1862)
Antietam (September 17, 1862)
Fredericksburg [in reserve] (December 13, 1862)
Chancellorsville (May 1-4, 1863)
2nd Winchester (June 14-15, 1863)
Gettysburg (July 1-3, 1863)
Bristoe Campaign (October 1863)
Mine Run Campaign (November-December 1863)
Payne's Farm (November 27, 1863)
The Wilderness (May 5-6, 1864)
Spotsylvania Court House (May 8-21, 1864)
North Anna (May 23-26, 1864)
Cold Harbor (June 1-3, 1864)
Lynchburg Campaign (May-June 1864)
Monocacy (July 9, 1864)
Kernstown (July 24, 1864)
Shepherdstown (August 25, 1864)
3rd Winchester (September 19, 1864)
Fisher's Hill (September 22, 1864)
Cedar Creek (October 19, 1864)
Petersburg Siege [detachment] (June 1864-April 1865)

Hatcher's Run (February 5-7, 1865)
Fort Stedman (March 25, 1865)
Petersburg Final Assault (April 2, 1865)
Sayler's Creek (April 6, 1865)
Appomattox Court House (April 9, 1865)
Further Reading: Jones, Terry L., *Lee's Tigers: The Louisiana Infantry in the Army of Northern Virginia*. Buckley, Cornelius M., S.J., translator, *A Frenchman, a Chaplain, a Rebel: The War Letters of Pere Louis-Hippolyte Gache, S.J.*.

153. LOUISIANA 11TH INFANTRY BATTALION

Organization: Organized with six companies at Monroe on May 14, 1862. Permanently consolidated with the Confederate Guards [Louisiana] Infantry Battalion and Crescent Infantry Regiment and designated as the Crescent Infantry Regiment on November 3, 1863.
First Commander: Jacob D. Shelley (Lieutenant Colonel)
Field Officer: James H. Beard (Major, Lieutenant Colonel)
Assignments: District of West Louisiana, Trans-Mississippi Department (July-October 1862)
Mouton's Brigade, District of West Louisiana, Trans-Mississippi Department (October 1862-November 1863)
Battle: Fort Beauregard (May 10-11, 1863)

154. LOUISIANA 11TH INFANTRY REGIMENT

Organization: Organized at Camp Moore on August 13, 1861. Mustered into Confederate service on August 18, 1861. Failed at reorganization in the spring of 1862. The regiment was disbanded with the men assigned to the 13th and 20th Infantry Regiments and the 14th Sharpshooters Battalion on August 19, 1862. Ordered to be reorganized by S.O. #222, Adjutant and Inspector General's Office, dated September 23, 1862. However, this was soon deemed to be impractical.
First Commander: Samuel F. Marks (Colonel)
Field Officers: Robert H. Barrow (Lieutenant Colonel)
Edward G. W. Butler, Jr. (Major)
Alexander Mason (Major)
James A. Ventress, Jr. (Major)
Assignments: McCown's Brigade, 1st Geographical Division, Department #2 (September-October 1861)
Marks' Brigade, McCown's Division, 1st Geographical Division, Department #2 (October 1861-February 1862)
Marks' Brigade, McCown's Command, Department #2 (February-March 1862)

Fort Pillow, Department #2 (March 1862)
Russell's Brigade, Clark's Division, 1st Corps, Army of the Mississippi, Department #2 (March-April 1862)
Mouton's Brigade, Ruggles' Division, 2nd Corps, Army of the Mississippi, Department #2 (April-June 1862)
Mouton's Brigade, 2nd Corps, Army of the Mississippi, Department #2 (June-July 1862)
Mouton's Brigade, Jones' Division, Army of the Mississippi, Department #2 (July-August 1862)
Battles: Belmont (November 7, 1861)
Island #10 (April 6-7, 1862)
Shiloh (April 6-7, 1862)
Corinth Campaign (April-June 1862)
Farmington (May 9, 1862)

155. LOUISIANA 12TH INFANTRY BATTALION

See: LOUISIANA CONFEDERATE GUARDS RESPONSE INFANTRY BATTALION

156. LOUISIANA 12TH INFANTRY REGIMENT

Organization: Organized with 12 companies at Camp Moore on August 13, 1861. Mustered into Confederate service on August 13, 1861. Surrendered by General Joseph E. Johnston at Durham Station, Orange County, North Carolina on April 26, 1865.
First Commander: Thomas M. Scott (Colonel)
Field Officers: James A. Boyd (Lieutenant Colonel)
John A. Dixon (Major)
Evander McN. Graham (Lieutenant Colonel)
Wade H. Hough (Lieutenant Colonel)
John C. Knott (Major)
Henry V. McCain (Major)
Noel L. Nelson (Major, Lieutenant Colonel, Colonel)
Thomas C. Standifer (Major, Lieutenant Colonel, Colonel)
Assignments: McCown's Brigade, 1st Geographical Division, Department #2 (September-October 1861)
Neely's Brigade, McCown's Division, 1st Geographical Division, Department #2 (October 1861-February 1862)
Neely's Brigade, McCown's Command, Department #2 (February-March 1862)
Fort Pillow, Army of the Mississippi, Department #2 (March-June 1862)
Grenada, Army of the Mississippi, Department #2 (June-July 1862)
3rd Sub-district, District of the Mississippi, Department #2 (July-August 1862)

1st Sub-district, District of the Mississippi, Department #2 (August 1862)
Scott's Brigade, Rust's Division, Loring's Corps, Army of West Tennessee, Department of Mississippi and East Louisiana (October-November 1862)
Scott's Brigade, Rust's Division, Loring's Corps, Army of North Mississippi, Department of Mississippi and East Louisiana (December 1862)
Scott's Brigade, Rust's Division, Loring's Corps, Army of the Department of Mississippi and East Louisiana (December 1862-January 1863)
Rust's Brigade, Loring's Division, Army of the Department of Mississippi and East Louisiana (January-February 1863)
Rust's Brigade, 3rd Military District, Department of Mississippi and East Louisiana (March-April 1863)
Buford's Brigade, Loring's Division, Department of Mississippi and East Louisiana (April-May 1863)
Buford's Brigade, Loring's Division, Department of the West (May-July 1863)
Buford's Brigade, Loring's Division, Department of Mississippi and East Louisiana (July 1863-January 1864)
Buford's-Scott's Brigade, Loring's Division, Department of Alabama, Mississippi, and East Louisiana (January-May 1864)
Scott's Brigade, Loring's Division, Army of Mississippi (May-July 1864)
Scott's Brigade, Loring's Division, 3rd Corps, Army of Tennessee (July 1864-April 1865)
Lowry's Brigade, Loring's Division, 3rd Corps, Army of Tennessee (April 1865)
Battles: Belmont [not engaged] (November 7, 1861)
Island #10 (March 4-5, 1862)
Island #10 (April 6-7, 1862)
Fort Pillow Bombardment (April 14, 1862)
Corinth (October 3-4, 1862)
Port Hudson Bombardment (March 14, 1863)
Grierson's Raid (April 17-May 2, 1863)
Vicksburg Campaign (May-July 1863)
Champion Hill (May 16, 1863)
Vicksburg Siege [detachment] (May-July 1863)
Jackson Siege (July 10-17, 1863)
Meridian Campaign (February-March 1864)
Atlanta Campaign (May-September 1864)
Resaca (May 14-15, 1864)
New Hope Church (May 25-June 4, 1864)
Kennesaw Mountain (June 27, 1864)
Peach Tree Creek (July 20, 1864)
Ezra Church (July 28, 1864)
Atlanta (July 22, 1864)

Atlanta Siege (July-September 1864)
Jonesboro (August 31-September 1, 1864)
Franklin (November 30, 1864)
Nashville (December 15-16, 1864)
Carolinas Campaign (February-April 1865)
Bentonville (March 19-21, 1865)
Further Reading: Eakin, Sue Lyles, and Morgan Peoples, eds., *"In Defense of My Country . . . ": The Civil War Letters of a Shiloh Confederate Soldier, Sergeant George Washington Bolton, and His Union Parish Neighbors of the Twelfth Regiment of Louisiana Volunteers (1861-1864).*

157. LOUISIANA 13TH INFANTRY BATTALION

See: LOUISIANA ORLEANS GUARD INFANTRY BATTALION

158. LOUISIANA 13TH INFANTRY REGIMENT

Organization: Organized at Camp Moore on September 9, 1861. Mustered into Confederate service on September 9, 1861. Consolidated with the 20th Infantry Regiment and designated as the 13th and 20th Consolidated Infantry Regiment on November 30, 1862. Reorganized at Mobile, Alabama in February 1865. Field consolidation with the 4th Infantry Regiment and 30th Infantry Battalion from February to April 1865. Consolidated with the 16th Infantry Regiment and designated as the Chalmette Consolidated Infantry Regiment in April 1865.
First Commander: Randall L. Gibson (Colonel)
Field Officers: Anatole P. Avegno (Major)
Francis L. Campbell (Major, Lieutenant Colonel, Colonel)
Edgar M. Dubroca (Major, Lieutenant Colonel)
Aristides Gerard (Lieutenant Colonel, Colonel)
Stephen O'Leary (Major)
Michael O. Tracy (Major)
Assignments: Cheatham's Brigade, 1st Geographical Division, Department #2 (September-October 1861)
Cheatham's Division, 1st Geographical Division, Department #2 (October 1861-March 1862)
Tappan's Brigade, 1st Grand Division, Army of the Mississippi, Department #2 (March 1862)
Tappan's Brigade, Clark's Division, 1st Grand Division, 2nd Corps, Army of the Mississippi, Department #2 (March 1862)
Gibson's Brigade, Ruggles' Division, 2nd Corps, Army of the Mississippi, Department #2 (March-April 1862)

Ruggles'-L. M. Walker's Brigade, Ruggles'-Anderson's Division, 2nd Corps, Army of the Mississippi, Department #2 (April-June 1862)
L. M. Walker's Brigade, 2nd Corps, Army of the Mississippi, Department #2 (June-July 1862)
L. M. Walker's Brigade, Jones'-Anderson's Division, Army of the Mississippi, Department #2 (July-August 1862)
D. W. Adams' Brigade, Anderson's Division, Army of the Mississippi, Department #2 (August 1862)
D. W. Adams' Brigade, Anderson's Division, Left Wing, Army of the Mississippi, Department #2 (August-November 1862)
D. W. Adams' Brigade, Anderson's Division, 2nd Corps, Army of Tennessee (November-December 1862)
Battles: Shiloh (April 6-7, 1862)
Perryville (October 8, 1862)
Murfreesboro (December 31, 1862-January 3, 1863)
Jackson Siege (July 10-17, 1863)
Chickamauga (September 19-20, 1863)
Chattanooga Siege (September-November 1863)
Chattanooga (November 23-25, 1863)
Mobile (March 17-April 12, 1865)

159. LOUISIANA 13TH AND 20TH CONSOLIDATED INFANTRY REGIMENT

Organization: Organized by the consolidation of the 13th and 20th Infantry Regiments at Shelbyville, Tennessee on November 30, 1862. Broken up at Mobile, Alabama in February 1865. The two regiments were recreated and promptly placed in new field consolidations.
First Commander: Randall L. Gibson (Colonel)
Field Officers: Samuel L. Bishop (Major)
Francis L. Campbell (Major, Lieutenant Colonel, Colonel)
Edgar M. Dubroca (Lieutenant Colonel)
Charles G. Guilett (Major)
Leon Von Zinken (Lieutenant Colonel, Colonel)
Assignments: D. W. Adams' Brigade, Anderson's Division, 2nd Corps, Army of Tennessee (November-December 1862)
D. W. Adams' Brigade, Breckinridge's Division, 2nd Corps, Army of Tennessee (December 1862-May 1863)
D. W. Adams' Brigade, Breckinridge's Division, Department of the West (May-July 1863)
D. W. Adams' Brigade, Breckinridge's Division, Department of Mississippi and East Louisiana (July-August 1863)

D. W. Adams' Brigade, Breckinridge's Division, 2nd Corps, Army of Tennessee (August-November 1863)
D. W. Adams'-Gibson's Brigade, Stewart's-Clayton's Division, 2nd Corps, Army of Tennessee (November 1863-February 1865)
Battles: Atlanta Campaign (May-September 1864)
New Hope Church (May 25-June 4, 1864)
Atlanta (July 22, 1864)
Ezra Church (July 28, 1864)
Atlanta Siege (July-September 1864)
Jonesboro (August 31-September 1, 1864)
Franklin (November 30, 1864)
Nashville (December 15-16, 1864)

160. LOUISIANA 14TH INFANTRY BATTALION, SHARPSHOOTERS

Organization: Organized from men of the 11th Infantry Regiment, which had failed to reorganize during the previous spring, with two companies at Camp Lookout, near Chattanooga, Tennessee on August 12, 1862. Surrendered by Lieutenant General Richard Taylor, commanding the Department of Alabama, Mississippi, and East Louisiana, at Citronelle, Alabama on May 4, 1865.
First Commander: John E. Austin (Major)
Assignments: D. W. Adams' Brigade, Anderson's Division, Army of the Mississippi, Department #2 (August 1862)
D. W. Adams' Brigade, Anderson's Division, Left Wing, Army of the Mississippi, Department #2 (August-November 1862)
D. W. Adams' Brigade, Anderson's Division, 2nd Corps, Army of Tennessee (November-December 1862)
D. W. Adams' Brigade, Breckinridge's Division, 2nd Corps, Army of Tennessee (December 1862-May 1863)
D. W. Adams' Brigade, Breckinridge's Division, Department of the West (May-July 1863)
D. W. Adams' Brigade, Breckinridge's Division, Department of Mississippi and East Louisiana (July-August 1863)
D. W. Adams' Brigade, Breckinridge's Division, 2nd Corps, Army of Tennessee (August-November 1863)
D. W. Adams'-Gibson's Brigade, Stewart's-Clayton's Division, 2nd Corps, Army of Tennessee (November 1863-January 1865)
Gibson's Brigade, District of the Gulf, Department of Alabama, Mississippi, and East Louisiana (March-April 1865)
Gibson's Brigade, Department of Alabama, Mississippi, and East Louisiana (April-May 1865)

Battles: Perryville (October 8, 1862)
Murfreesboro (December 31, 1862-January 3, 1863)
Jackson Siege (July 10-17, 1863)
Chickamauga (September 19-20, 1863)
Chattanooga Siege (September-November 1863)
Chattanooga (November 23-25, 1863)
Atlanta Campaign (May-September 1864)
New Hope Church (May 25-June 4, 1864)
Atlanta (July 22, 1864)
Ezra Church (July 28, 1864)
Atlanta Siege (July-September 1864)
Jonesboro (August 31-September 1, 1864)
Franklin (November 30, 1864)
Nashville (December 15-16, 1864)
Mobile (March 17-April 12, 1865)

161. LOUISIANA 14TH INFANTRY REGIMENT

Nickname: 1st Regiment, Polish Brigade

Organization: Organized as the 1st Polish Regiment on June 16, 1861. Mustered into Confederate service for the war at Camp Pulaski, near Amite, on August 24, 1861. Designation changed to the 13th Infantry Regiment on August 24, 1861. Designation changed to the 14th Infantry Regiment on September 21, 1861. Surrendered at Appomattox Court House, Virginia on April 9, 1865.

First Commander: Valery Sulakowski (Colonel)

Field Officers: Richard W. Jones (Lieutenant Colonel, Colonel)
William H. Toler (Major, Lieutenant Colonel)
Zebulon York (Major, Lieutenant Colonel, Colonel)
David Zable (Major, Lieutenant Colonel, Colonel)

Assignments: Department of the Peninsula (September-October 1861)
Sulakowski's Brigade, Department of the Peninsula (October 1861)
Rains' Division, Department of the Peninsula (January-April 1862)
Pryor's Brigade, Longstreet's Division, Department of Northern Virginia (April-June 1862)
Pryor's Brigade, Longstreet's Division, 1st Corps, Army of Northern Virginia (June-July 1862)
2nd Louisiana Brigade, Ewell's Division, 2nd Corps, Army of Northern Virginia (July 1862)
2nd Louisiana Brigade, A. P. Hill's Division, 2nd Corps, Army of Northern Virginia (July 1862)

2nd Louisiana Brigade, Ewell's Division, 2nd Corps, Army of Northern Virginia (August-September 1862)
1st Louisiana Brigade, Ewell's-Early's Division, 2nd Corps, Army of Northern Virginia (December 1862-May 1864)
Consolidated Louisiana Brigade, Early's-Gordon's Division, 2nd Corps, Army of Northern Virginia (May-June 1864)
Consolidated Louisiana Brigade, Gordon's Division, Valley District, Department of Northern Virginia (June-December 1864)
Consolidated Louisiana Brigade, Gordon's Division, 2nd Corps, Army of Northern Virginia (December 1864-April 1865)
Battles: Yorktown Siege (April-May 1862)
Williamsburg (May 5, 1862)
Seven Pines (May 31-June 1, 1862)
Seven Days Battles (June 25-July 1, 1862)
Mechanicsville (June 26, 1862)
Gaines' Mill (June 27, 1862)
Frayser's Farm (June 30, 1862)
Cedar Mountain (August 9, 1862)
Bristoe Station (August 26, 1862)
Kettle Run (August 27, 1862)
2nd Bull Run (August 28-30, 1862)
Chantilly (September 1, 1862)
Harpers Ferry (September 12-15, 1862)
Antietam (September 17, 1862)
Fredericksburg (December 13, 1862)
Chancellorsville (May 1-4, 1863)
2nd Winchester (June 14-15, 1863)
Gettysburg (July 1-3, 1863)
Bristoe Campaign (October 1863)
Mine Run Campaign (November-December 1863)
Payne's Farm (November 27, 1863)
The Wilderness (May 5-6, 1864)
Spotsylvania Court House (May 8-21, 1864)
North Anna (May 23-26, 1864)
Cold Harbor (June 1-3, 1864)
Lynchburg Campaign (May-June 1864)
Monocacy (July 9, 1864)
Kernstown (July 24, 1864)
Shepherdstown (August 25, 1864)
3rd Winchester (September 19, 1864)
Fisher's Hill (September 22, 1864)

Cedar Creek (October 19, 1864)
Petersburg Siege [from December] (June 1864-April 1865)
Hatcher's Run (February 5-7, 1865)
Fort Stedman (March 25, 1865)
Petersburg Final Assault (April 2, 1865)
Sayler's Creek (April 6, 1865)
Appomattox Court House (April 9, 1865)
Further Reading: Jones, Terry L., *Lee's Tigers: The Louisiana Infantry in the Army of Northern Virginia.* Sheeran, James B., *Confederate Chaplain: A War Journal.*

162. LOUISIANA 15TH INFANTRY BATTALION, SHARPSHOOTERS

Organization: Organized with five companies from those members of Miles' Legion, Infantry Battalion west of the Mississippi River ca. July 1864. Surrendered by General E. K. Smith, commanding Trans-Mississippi Department, on May 26, 1865.
First Commander: Robert C. Weatherly (Major)
Assignments: Thomas' Brigade, Polignac's Division, District of West Louisiana, Trans-Mississippi Department (August-October 1864)
1st (Thomas') Louisiana Brigade, 2nd (Polignac's-Thomas') Division, 1st Corps, Trans-Mississippi Department (October 1864-May 1865)

163. LOUISIANA 15TH INFANTRY REGIMENT

Nickname: 2nd Regiment, Polish Brigade
Organization: Organized by the addition of two companies of the 7th Louisiana Infantry Battalion to the 3rd Infantry Battalion to form a regiment near Richmond, Virginia on July 24, 1862. Field consolidation with the 10th Infantry Regiment in 1864 and 1865. Surrendered at Appomattox Court House, Virginia on April 9, 1865.
First Commander: Francis T. Nicholls (Colonel)
Field Officers: Andrew Brady (Major)
McGavock Goodwyn (Major, Lieutenant Colonel)
Edmund Pendleton (Colonel)
Robert A. Wilkinson (Major, Lieutenant Colonel)
Assignments: J. R. Anderson's Brigade, A. P. Hill's Division, 1st Corps, Army of Northern Virginia (July 1862)
2nd Louisiana Brigade, McLaws' Division, 1st Corps, Army of Northern Virginia (July 1862)
2nd Louisiana Brigade, A. P. Hill's Division, 2nd Corps, Army of Northern Virginia (July 1862)

2nd Louisiana Brigade, Jackson's-Trimble's Division, 2nd Corps, Army of Northern Virginia (August 1862-May 1864)

Consolidated Louisiana Brigade, Early's-Gordon's Division, 2nd Corps, Army of Northern Virginia (May-June 1864)

Consolidated Louisiana Brigade, Gordon's Division, Valley District, Department of Northern Virginia (June-December 1864)

Consolidated Louisiana Brigade, Gordon's Division, 2nd Corps, Army of Northern Virginia (December 1864-April 1865)

Battles: Cedar Mountain (August 9, 1862)

Groveton (August 28, 1862)

2nd Bull Run (August 28-30, 1862)

Harpers Ferry (September 12-15, 1862)

Antietam (September 17, 1862)

Fredericksburg [not engaged] (December 13, 1862)

Chancellorsville (May 1-4, 1863)

2nd Winchester (June 14-15, 1863)

Gettysburg (July 1-3, 1863)

Bristoe Campaign (October 1863)

Mine Run Campaign (November-December 1863)

Payne's Farm (November 27, 1863)

The Wilderness (May 5-6, 1864)

Spotsylvania Court House (May 8-21, 1864)

North Anna (May 23-26, 1864)

Cold Harbor (June 1-3, 1864)

Lynchburg Campaign (May-June 1864)

Monocacy (July 9, 1864)

Kernstown (July 24, 1864)

Shepherdstown (August 25, 1864)

3rd Winchester (September 19, 1864)

Fisher's Hill (September 22, 1864)

Cedar Creek (October 19, 1864)

Petersburg Siege [from December] (June 1864-April 1865)

Hatcher's Run (February 5-7, 1865)

Fort Stedman (March 25, 1865)

Petersburg Final Assault (April 2, 1865)

Sayler's Creek (April 6, 1865)

Appomattox Court House (April 9, 1865)

Further Reading: Jones, Terry L., *Lee's Tigers: The Louisiana Infantry in the Army of Northern Virginia.*

164. LOUISIANA 16TH INFANTRY BATTALION

See: LOUISIANA CONFEDERATE GUARDS RESPONSE INFANTRY BATTALION

165. LOUISIANA 16TH INFANTRY REGIMENT

Organization: Organized at Camp Moore on September 29, 1861. Mustered into Confederate service on September 29, 1861. Consolidation with the 25th Infantry Regiment and designated as the 16th and 25th Consolidated Infanty Regiment on November 30, 1862. Field consolidation with the 20th Infantry Regiment and the 1st Infantry Regiment Regulars from February to April 1865. Consolidated with the 13th Infantry Regiment and designated as the Chalmette Consolidated Infantry Regiment in April 1865.

First Commander: Preston Pond, Jr. (Colonel)

Field Officers: Daniel C. Gober (Major, Colonel)
Robert H. Lindsay (Major, Lieutenant Colonel)
Enoch Mason (Lieutenant Colonel)
Robert P. Oliver (Major)
Frank M. Raxsdale (Major)
William E. Walker (Lieutenant Colonel)

Assignments: Department #1 (September 1861-March 1862)
Pond's Brigade, 1st (Ruggles') Corps, 2nd Grand Division, Army of the Mississippi, Department #2 (March 1862)
Pond's Brigade, Ruggles' Division, 2nd Corps, Army of the Mississippi, Department #2 (March-April 1862)
Mouton's Brigade, Ruggles'-Anderson's Division, 2nd Corps, Army of the Mississippi, Department #2 (April-June 1862)
Mouton's Brigade, 2nd Corps, Army of the Mississippi, Department #2 (June-July 1862)
Mouton's Brigade, Anderson's Division, Army of the Mississippi, Department #2 (July-August 1862)
D. W. Adams' Brigade, Anderson's Division, Army of the Mississippi, Department #2 (August 1862)
D. W. Adams' Brigade, Anderson's Division, Left Wing, Army of the Mississippi, Department #2 (August-November 1862)
D. W. Adams' Brigade, Anderson's Division, 2nd Corps, Army of Tennessee (November 1862)
Gibson's Brigade, District of the Gulf, Department of Alabama, Mississippi, and East Louisiana (February-April 1865)
Gibson's Brigade, Department of Alabama, Mississippi, and East Louisiana (April-May 1865)

Battles: Shiloh (April 6-7, 1862)
Corinth Campaign (April-June 1862)

Farmington (May 9, 1862)
Kentucky Campaign (August-October 1862)
Perryville (October 8, 1862)
Mobile (March 17-April 12, 1865)
Spanish Fort (March 27-April 8, 1865)

166. LOUISIANA 16TH AND 25TH CONSOLIDATED INFANTRY REGIMENT

Organization: Organized by the consolidation of the 16th and 25th Infantry Regiments at Shelbyville, Tennessee on November 30, 1862. Broken up at Mobile, Alabama on February 3, 1865. The two regiments resumed their original designations.
First Commander: Stuart W. Fisk (Colonel)
Field Officers: Daniel C. Gober (Colonel)
J. C. Lewis (Colonel)
Robert H. Lindsay (Lieutenant Colonel)
Calvin H. Moore (Major, Lieutenant Colonel)
Frank C. Zacharie (Major, Lieutenant Colonel, Colonel)
Assignments: D. W. Adams' Brigade, Anderson's Division, 2nd Corps, Army of Tennessee (November-December 1862)
D. W. Adams' Brigade, Breckinridge's Division, 2nd Corps, Army of Tennessee (December 1862-May 1863)
D. W. Adams' Brigade, Breckinridge's Division, Department of the West (May-July 1863)
D. W. Adams' Brigade, Breckinridge's Division, Department of Mississippi and East Louisiana (July-August 1863)
D. W. Adams' Brigade, Breckinridge's Division, 2nd Corps, Army of Tennessee (August-November 1863)
D. W. Adams'-Gibson's Brigade, Stewart's-Clayton's Division, 2nd Corps, Army of Tennessee (November 1863-February 1865)
Gibson's Brigade, District of the Gulf, Department of Alabama, Mississippi, and East Louisiana (February 1865)
Battles: Murfreesboro (December 31, 1862-January 3, 1863)
Jackson Siege (July 10-17, 1863)
Chickamauga (September 19-20, 1863)
Chattanooga Siege (September-November 1863)
Chattanooga (November 23-25, 1863)
Atlanta Campaign (May-September 1864)
Mill Creek Gap (May 8, 1864)
Resaca (May 14-15, 1864)
New Hope Church (May 25-June 4, 1864)

Atlanta (July 22, 1864)
Ezra Church (July 28, 1864)
Atlanta Siege (July-September 1864)
Jonesboro (August 31-September 1, 1864)
Florence (October 30, 1864)
Franklin (November 30, 1864)
Nashville (December 15-16, 1864)

167. LOUISIANA 17TH INFANTRY BATTALION

See: LOUISIANA 9TH INFANTRY BATTALION

168. LOUISIANA 17TH INFANTRY REGIMENT

Organization: Organized at Camp Moore on September 29, 1861. Mustered into Confederate service at Camp Moore on September 29, 1861. Regiment surrendered at Vicksburg, Warren County, Mississippi on July 4, 1863. Paroled at Vicksburg, Warren County, Mississippi in July 1863. Those members of the regiment east of the Mississippi River was consolidated with similar portions of the 3rd, 21st (Smith's-Higgins'-Patton's), 22nd (Theard's-Herrick's), 26th, 27th, 29th and 31st Infantry Regiments and designated as the 22nd Consolidated Infantry Regiment at Enterprise, Mississippi on January 26, 1864. They became part of Company G, of that regiment. The balance of the regiment was reorganized at Minden, Louisiana in May 1864. Surrendered by General E. K. Smith, commanding Trans-Mississippi Department, on May 26, 1865.
First Commander: S. S. Heard (Colonel)
Field Officers: Charles Jones (Lieutenant Colonel)
Robert B. Jones (Major)
William A. Maddox (Major)
William A. Redditt (Major, Lieutenant Colonel)
Robert Richardson (Colonel)
Madison Rogers (Lieutenant Colonel)
David W. Self (Major)
Assignments: Ruggles' Brigade, Department #1 (September 1861-February 1862)
Ruggles' Brigade, Department #2 (February-March 1862)
Pond's Brigade, 1st Corps, 2nd Grand Division, Army of the Mississippi, Department #2 (March 1862)
Anderson's Brigade, Ruggles'-Anderson's Division, 2nd Corps, Army of the Mississippi, Department #2 (March-May 1862)
Smith's Brigade, District of the Mississippi, Department #2 (June-July 1862)
2nd/3rd Sub-district, District of the Mississippi, Department #2 (July-October 1862)

Department of Mississippi and East Louisiana (October 1862)
2nd Military District, Department of Mississippi and East Louisiana (October-December 1862)
Thomas' Brigade, Lee's Provisional Division, 2nd Military District, Department of Mississippi and East Louisiana (December 1862)
Unattached, 2nd Military District, Department of Mississippi and East Louisiana (December 1862-January 1863)
Lee's Brigade, Smith's Division, 2nd Military District, Department of Mississippi and East Louisiana (January-February 1863)
Baldwin's Brigade, Smith's Division, 2nd Military District, Department of Mississippi and East Louisiana (March-April 1863)
Baldwin's Brigade, Smith's Division, Department of Mississippi and East Louisiana (April-July 1863)
Thomas' Brigade, Polignac's Division, District of West Louisiana, Trans-Mississippi Department (May-September 1864)
1st (Thomas') Louisiana Brigade, 2nd (Polignac's-Thomas') Division, 1st Corps, Trans-Mississippi Department (September 1864-May 1865)
Battles: Shiloh (April 6-7, 1862)
Corinth Campaign (April-June 1862)
Vicksburg Bombardments (May 18-July 27, 1862)
Chickasaw Bayou (December 27-29, 1862)
Vicksburg Campaign (May-July 1863)
Port Gibson (May 1, 1863)
Vicksburg Siege (May-July 1863)
Further Reading: Small, J. A., *Memories of the Civil War As Remembered By an Old Veteran.*

169. LOUISIANA 18TH INFANTRY REGIMENT

Organization: Organization begun with seven companies at Camp Moore, near New Orleans on October 5, 1861. Mustered into Confederate service on October 5, 1861. Organization completed at Camp Benjamin in January 1862. Consolidated with the 10th Infantry Battalion and designated as the 18th Consolidated Infantry Regiment at Simmesport on November 14, 1863.
First Commander: J. J. A. Alfred Mouton (Colonel)
Field Officers: Leopold L. Armant (Major, Colonel)
Louis Bush (Major, Lieutenant Colonel)
Joseph Collins (Major)
Joseph K. Gourdain (Major)
Paul B. Leeds (Major)
William Mouton (Major)
Alfred Roman (Lieutenant Colonel, Colonel)

Assignments: Department #1 (October 1861-February 1862)
Ruggles' Brigade, Department #2 (February-March 1862)
Mouton's Brigade, 1st Corps, 2nd Grand Division, Army of the Mississippi, Department #2 (March 1862)
Pond's Brigade, Ruggles' Division, 2nd Corps, Army of the Mississippi, Department #2 (March-April 1862)
Mouton's Brigade, Cheatham's-Ruggles Division, 2nd Corps, Army of the Mississippi, Department #2 (April-June 1862)
Mouton's-Reichard's Brigade, 2nd Corps, Army of the Mississippi, Department #2 (June-July 1862)
Reichard's Brigade, Jones' Division, Army of the Mississippi, Department #2 (July 1862)
District of the Gulf, Department #2 (August-October 1862)
Mouton's Brigade, District of West Louisiana, Trans-Mississippi Department (October 1862-November 1863)
Battles: Pittsburg Landing (March 1, 1862)
Purdy Expedition and Crump's Landing operations [detachment] (March 9-14, 1862)
Shiloh (April 6-7, 1862)
Corinth Campaign (April-June 1862)
Georgia Landing, near Labadieville (October 27, 1862)
Bayou Teche (January 14, 1863)
Fort Bisland (April 13-14, 1863)
Further Reading: Bergeron, Arthur W., Jr., ed., *Reminiscences of Uncle Silas: The History of the Eighteenth Louisiana Infantry Regiment.*

170. LOUISIANA 18TH CONSOLIDATED INFANTRY REGIMENT

Organization: Organized by the consolidation of the 10th Infantry Battalion and the 18th Infantry Regiment at Simmesport, Louisiana on November 14, 1863. Surrendered by General E. K. Smith, commanding Trans-Mississippi Department, on May 26, 1865.
First Commander: Leopold L. Armant (Colonel)
Field Officers: Joseph Collins (Lieutenant Colonel, Colonel)
Joseph K Gourdain (Major)
William Mouton (Major, Lieutenant Colonel)
Assignments: Mouton's-Gray's Brigade, Mouton's-Polignac's Division, District of West Louisiana, Trans-Mississippi Department (November 1863-September 1864)
2nd (Gray's) Louisiana Brigade, 2nd (Polignac's) Division, 1st Corps, Trans-Mississippi Department (September 1864-May 1865)
Battles: Red River Campaign (May 10-22, 1864)

Mansfield (April 8, 1864)
Pleasant Hill (April 9, 1864)
Yellow Bayou (May 18, 1864)
Further Reading: Bergeron, Arthur W., Jr., ed., *Reminiscences of Uncle Silas: The History of the Eighteenth Louisiana Infantry Regiment.*

171. LOUISIANA 19TH INFANTRY BATTALION

See: LOUISIANA 7TH INFANTRY BATTALION

172. LOUISIANA 19TH INFANTRY REGIMENT

Organization: Organized with eight companies at Camp Moore on November 19, 1861. Two additional companies were assigned on December 11, 1861. Consolidated with the 4th Infantry Battalion, 20th, and 25th Infantry Regiments and designated as Companies A, D, and E, Pelican Consolidated Infantry Regiment in April 1865.
First Commander: Benjamin L. Hodge (Colonel)
Field Officers: Loudon Butler (Major, Lieutenant Colonel)
Camp Flournoy (Major)
James M. Hollingsworth (Lieutenant Colonel)
Hyder A. Kennedy (Major, Lieutenant Colonel)
Winfrey B. Scott (Major)
Richard W. Turner (Major, Lieutenant Colonel, Colonel)
Wesley P. Winans (Major, Lieutenant Colonel, Colonel)
Assignments: Department #1 (November 1861-February 1862)
Pond's Brigade, 1st Corps, 2nd Grand Division, Army of the Mississippi, Department #2 (March 1862)
Gibson's Brigade, Ruggles' Division, 2nd Corps, Army of the Mississippi, Department #2 (April 1862)
Mouton's Brigade, Cheatham's-Ruggles' Division, 2nd Corps, Army of the Mississippi, Department #2 (April-June 1862)
Mouton's-Reichard's Brigade, 2nd Corps, Army of the Mississippi, Department #2 (June-July 1862)
Reichard's Brigade, Jones' Division, Army of the Mississippi, Department #2 (July 1862)
District of the Gulf, Department #2 (July-September 1862)
Detachment of Observation [Tattnall's], District of the Gulf, Department #2 (October-November 1862)
District of the Gulf, Department #2 (November 1862-April 1863)
Eastern Division, Department of the Gulf (April-May 1863)
D. W. Adams'-Reichard's Brigade, Breckinridge's Division, Department of the West (May-July 1863)

D. W. Adams'-Gibson's Brigade, Breckinridge's Division, Department of Mississippi and East Louisiana (July-August 1863)
D. W. Adams'-Gibson's Brigade, Breckinridge's Division, 2nd Corps, Army of Tennessee (September-November 1863)
D. W. Adams'-Gibson's Brigade, Stewart's-Clayton's Division, 2nd Corps, Army of Tennessee (November 1863-February 1865)
Gibson's Brigade, District of the Gulf, Department of Alabama, Mississippi, and East Louisiana (February-April 1865)
Battles: Shiloh (April 6-7, 1862)
Corinth Campaign (April-June 1862)
Jackson Siege (July 10-17, 1863)
Chickamauga (September 19-20, 1863)
Chattanooga Siege (September-November 1863)
Chattanooga (November 23-25, 1863)
Atlanta Campaign (May-September 1864)
Mill Creek Gap (May 8-11, 1864)
Resaca (May 14-15, 1864)
New Hope Church (May 25-June 4, 1864)
Atlanta (July 22, 1864)
Ezra Church (July 28, 1864)
Atlanta Siege (July-September 1864)
Ezra Church (July 28, 1864)
Jonesboro (August 31-September 1, 1864)
Nashville (December 15-16, 1864)
Mobile (March 17-April 12, 1865)

173. LOUISIANA 20TH INFANTRY REGIMENT

Nickname: Lovell Regiment
Organization: Organized by the increase of the 6th (Reichard's) Infantry Battalion to a regiment at Camp Lewis, New Orleans on January 3, 1862. Consolidated with the 13th Infantry Regiment and designated as the 13th and 20th Consolidated Infantry Regiment from November 30, 1862. Reorganized at Mobile, Alabama on February 3, 1865. Field consolidation with 16th Infantry Regiment and 1st Infantry Regiment Regulars from February to April 1865. Consolidated with the 4th Infantry Battalion, 19th, and 25th Infantry Regiments and designated as the Pelican Consolidated Infantry Regiment, as Company H in April 1865.
First Commander: Augustus Reichard (Colonel)
Field Officers: Samuel L. Bishop (Major, Lieutenant Colonel)
Samuel Boyd (Lieutenant Colonel)
Charles G. Guillet (Major)

Leon Von Zinken (Major, Lieutenant Colonel, Colonel)
Assignments: Department #1 (February-March 1862)
Anderson's Brigade, 1st Corps, 2nd Grand Division, Army of the Mississippi, Department #2 (March 1862)
Anderson's Brigade, Ruggles' Division, 2nd Corps, Army of the Mississippi, Department #2 (March-April 1862)
Ruggles' Brigade, Cheatham's-Ruggles' Division, 2nd Corps, Army of the Mississippi, Department #2 (April-June 1862)
Mouton's-Reichard's Brigade, 2nd Corps, Army of the Mississippi, Department #2 (June-July 1862)
Mouton's-Reichard's Brigade, Jones' Division, Army of the Mississippi, Department #2 (July-August 1862)
Mouton's-Reichard's-D. W. Adams' Brigade, Jones'-Anderson's Division, Left Wing, Army of the Mississippi, Department #2 (August-November 1862)
D. W. Adams' Brigade, Anderson's Division, 2nd Corps, Army of Tennessee (November-December 1862)
Gibson's Brigade, District of the Gulf, Department of Alabama, Mississippi, and East Louisiana (February-April 1865)
Battles: Shiloh (April 6-7, 1862)
Corinth Campaign (April-June 1862)
Monterey (April 29, 1862)
Farmington (May 9, 1862)
Perryville (October 8, 1862)
Mobile (March 17-April 12, 1865)
Spanish Fort (March 27-April 8, 1865)

174. LOUISIANA 21ST (KENNEDY'S) INFANTRY REGIMENT

Nicknames: Jackson Regiment,
Organization: Organized by the increase of the 5th Infantry Battalion to a regiment at Columbus, Kentucky on February 9, 1862. Broken up on July 28, 1862. Ordered to be reorganized by S.O. #222, Adjutant and Inspector General's Office, dated September 23, 1862. However, this was soon deemed to be impractical.
First Commander: John B. G. Kennedy (Colonel)
Field Officers: John Newman (Major)
West Steever (Lieutenant Colonel)
Assignments: Marks' Brigade, McCown's Division, 1st Geographical Division, Department #2 (February 1862)
Fort Pillow, Department #2 (March-May 1862)
L. M. Walker's Brigade, J. P. Anderson's Division, 2nd Corps, Army of the Mississippi, Department #2 (May-June 1862)

L. M. Walker's Brigade, 2nd Corps, Army of the Mississippi, Department #2 (June-July 1862)

L. M. Walker's Brigade, S. Jones' Division, Army of the Mississippi, Department #2 (July-August 1862)

Battles: Island #10 (April 6-7, 1862)

Bridge Creek [skirmish] (May 27, 1862)

175. LOUISIANA 21ST (SMITH'S-HIGGINS'-PATTON'S) INFANTRY REGIMENT

Also Known As: 22nd Infantry Regiment

Organization: Organized as the 22nd Infantry Regiment at New Orleans on March 28, 1862. This regiment served as heavy artillery throughout its existance. Reorganized with four companies at Camp Moore on May 24, 1862. Reduced to two companies in July 1862. The four companies were reconstituted in November 1862. Increased to five companies in December 1862. Designated as the 21st Infantry Regiment ca. January 1863. Regiment surrendered at Vicksburg, Warren County, Mississippi on July 4, 1863. Paroled at Vicksburg, Warren County, Mississippi in July 1863. Declared exchanged on September 12, 1863. Consolidated with those portions of the 3rd, 17th, 22nd (Theard's-Herrick's), 26th, 27th, 29th, amd 31st Infantry Regiments east of the Mississippi River and designated as the 22nd Consolidated Infantry Regiment at Enterprise, Mississippi on January 26, 1864. This regiment became Companies I & K of the new regiment.

First Commander: Martin L. Smith (Colonel)

Field Officers: Edward Higgins (Lieutenant Colonel, Colonel)

Edward Ivy (Major, Lieutenant Colonel)

Isaac W. Patton (Colonel)

John T. Plattsmier (Lieutenant Colonel)

George Purves (Major)

Richard L Robertson (Major)

Assignments: Coast Defenses, Department #1 (March-May 1862)

Department #1 (May 1862)

Defenses of Vicksburg, Department #1 (May-June 1862)

Department of Southern Mississippi and East Louisiana (June-July 1862)

2nd/3rd Sub-district, District of the Mississippi, Department #2 (July-October 1862)

Department of Mississippi and East Louisiana (October 1862)

2nd Military District, Department of Mississippi and East Louisiana (October-December 1862)

Higgins' Brigade, Lee's Provisional Division, 2nd Military District, Department of Mississippi and East Louisiana (December 1862)

Lee's Brigade, 2nd Military District, Department of Mississippi and East Louisiana (December 1862-January 1863)
Lee's Brigade, Smith's Division, 2nd Military District, Department of Mississippi and East Louisiana (January-February 1863)
Hébert's Brigade, Maury's Division, 2nd Military District, Department of Mississippi and East Louisiana (March-April 1863)
Hébert's Brigade, Maury's Division, Department of Mississippi and East Louisiana (April-July 1863)
Mackall's Brigade, Forney's Division (November 1863-January 1864)
Battles: New Orleans (April 18-25, 1862)
Vicksburg Bombardments (May 18-July 27, 1862)
Chickasaw Bayou (December 27-29, 1862)
Snyder's Mill (December 27, 1862)
Fort Pemberton (March 11, 1863)
Fort Pemberton (March 13, 1863)
Fort Pemberton (March 16, 1863)
Fort Pemberton (April 2, 1863)
Fort Pemberton (April 4, 1863)
Snyder's Bluff (April 30-May 1, 1863)
Vicksburg Campaign (May-July 1863)
Vicksburg Siege (May-July 1863)

176. LOUISIANA 22ND (THEARD'S-HERRICK'S) INFANTRY REGIMENT

Also Known As: 23rd Infantry Regiment
Organization: Organized as the 23rd Infantry Regiment in New Orleans in January 1862. Mustered into Confederate service in March 1862. Reorganized with four companies on May 25, 1862. Designation changed to 22nd (Theard's-Herrick's) Infantry Regiment in early 1863. This regiment generally served as heavy artillery. Regiment surrendered at Vicksburg, Warren County, Mississippi on July 4, 1863. Paroled at Vicksburg, Warren County, Mississippi in July 1863. Consolidated with those portions east of the Mississippi River of the 3rd, 17th, 21st (Smith's-Higgins'-Patton's), 26th, 27th, 29th, and 31st Infantry Regiments and designated as the 22nd Infantry Regiment Consolidated at Enterprise, Mississippi on January 26, 1864. It was assigned as Companies A, B, C, D, and E of the new unit.
First Commander: Paul E. Theard (Colonel)
Field Officers: Charles H. Herrick (Colonel)
Samuel Jones (Major, Lieutenant Colonel)
William S. Lovell (Lieutenant Colonel)
Washington F. Marks (Major)

Aristee L. Tissot (Lieutenant Colonel)
Assignments: Coast Defenses, Department #1 (January-May 1862)
Department #1 (May 1862)
Defenses of Vicksburg, Department #1 (June 1862)
Department of Southern Mississippi and East Louisiana (June-July 1862)
2nd/3rd Sub-district, District of the Mississippi, Department #2 (July-October 1862)
Department of Mississippi and East Louisiana (October 1862)
River Batteries, 2nd Military District, Department of Mississippi and East Louisiana (October 1862-April 1863)
River Batteries, Department of Mississippi and East Louisiana (April-July 1863)
Mackall's Brigade, Forney's Division (November 1863-January 1864)
Battles: New Orleans (April 18-25, 1862)
Vicksburg Bombardments (May 18-July 27, 1862)
Fort Pemberton (March 1863)
Vicksburg Passage (April 16, 1863)
Vicksburg Campaign (May-July 1863)
Vicksburg Siege (May-July 1863)

177. LOUISIANA 22ND CONSOLIDATED INFANTRY REGIMENT

Organization: Organized by the consolidation of those members of the 3rd, 17th, 21st (Smith's-Higgins'-Patton's), 22nd (Theard's-Herrick's), 26th, 27th, 29th, and 31st Infantry Regiments east of the Mississippi River at Enterprise, Mississippi on January 26, 1864. It served as heavy artillery during most of its service. Surrendered by Lieutenant General Richard Taylor, commanding the Department of Alabama, Mississippi, and East Louisiana, at Citronelle, Alabama on May 4, 1865.
First Commander: Isaac W. Patton (Colonel)
Field Officers: Joseph O. Landry (Lieutenant Colonel)
Washington F. Marks (Major)
Assignments: Fuller's Artillery Brigade, District of the Gulf, Department of Alabama, Mississippi, and East Louisiana (February-May 1864)
Patton's Brigade, District of the Gulf, Department of Alabama, Mississippi, and East Louisiana (June-August 1864)
Higgins' Brigade, District of the Gulf, Department of Alabama, Mississippi, and East Louisiana (September-October 1864)
Baker's Brigade, Liddell's Division, District of the Gulf, Department of Alabama, Mississippi, and East Louisiana (October-December 1864)
Burnet's Command, Artillery Reserves, etc., District of the Gulf, Department of Alabama, Mississippi, and East Louisiana (March-April 1865)

Burnet's Command, Department of Alabama, Mississippi, and East Louisiana (April-May 1865)
Battles: Mobile (March 17-April 12, 1865)
Spanish Fort (March 27-April 8, 1865)

178. LOUISIANA 23RD INFANTRY REGIMENT

See: LOUISIANA 22ND (THEARD'S-HERRICK'S) INFANTRY REGIMENT

179. LOUISIANA 24TH INFANTRY REGIMENT

See: LOUISIANA CRESCENT INFANTRY REGIMENT AND LOUISIANA CRESCENT CONSOLIDATED INFANTRY REGIMENT

180. LOUISIANA 25TH INFANTRY REGIMENT

Organization: Organized at New Orleans on March 26, 1862. Consolidated with the 16th Infantry Regiment and designated as the 16th and 25th Consolidated Infantry Regiment on November 30, 1862. Reorganized on February 3, 1865. Field consolidation with the 4th Infantry Battalion from February to April 1865. Consolidated with the 19th, 20th, and 25th Infantry Regiments and designated as Companies B and C, Pelican Consolidated Infantry Regiment in April 1865.
First Commander: Stuart W. Fisk (Colonel)
Field Officers: Joseph C. Lewis (Lieutenant Colonel, Colonel)
Calvin H. Moore (Major, Lieutenant Colonel)
Francis C. Zacharie (Major, Lieutenant Colonel, Colonel)
Assignments: Department #1 (March 1862)
Anderson's Brigade, Cheatham's-Ruggles' Division, 2nd Corps, Army of the Mississippi, Department #2 (April-June 1862)
Anderson's Brigade, 2nd Corps, Army of the Mississippi, Department #2 (June-July 1862)
Anderson's Brigade, Jones' Division, Army of the Mississippi, Department #2 (July-August 1862)
D. W. Adams' Brigade, Anderson's Division, Left Wing, Army of the Mississippi, Department #2 (August-November 1862)
D. W. Adams' Brigade, Anderson's Division, 2nd Corps, Army of Tennessee (November-December 1862)
D. W. Adams' Brigade, Breckinridge's Division, 2nd Corps, Army of Tennessee (December 1862-May 1863)
D. W. Adams' Brigade, Breckinridge's Division, Department of the West (May-July 1863)
D. W. Adams' Brigade, Breckinridge's Division, Department of Mississippi and East Louisiana (July-August 1863)

D. W. Adams' Brigade, Breckinridge's Division, 2nd Corps, Army of Tennessee (August-November 1863)
D. W. Adams'-Gibson's Brigade, Stewart's-Clayton's Division, 2nd Corps, Army of Tennessee (November 1863-January 1865)
Gibson's Brigade, District of the Gulf, Department of Alabama, Mississippi, and East Louisiana (March-April 1865)
Battles: Corinth Campaign (April-June 1862)
Farmington (May 9, 1862)
Perryville (October 8, 1862)
Mobile (March 17-April 12, 1865)
Spanish Fort (March 27-April 8, 1865)

181. LOUISIANA 26TH INFANTRY REGIMENT

Organization: Organized at Camp Lovell, Berwick City on April 3, 1862. Regiment surrendered at Vicksburg, Warren County, Mississippi on July 4, 1863. Paroled at Vicksburg, Warren County, Mississippi in July 1863. Those members of the regiment east of the Mississippi River was consolidated with similar portions of the 3rd, 17th, 21st (Smith's-Higgins'-Patton's), 22nd (Theard's-Herrick's), 27th, 29th and 31st Infantry Regiments and designated as the 22nd Consolidated Infantry Regiment at Enterprise, Mississippi on January 26, 1864. They became part of Company F, of that regiment. Surrendered by General E. K. Smith, commanding Trans-Mississippi Department, on May 26, 1865.
First Commander: Alexander E. DeClouet (Colonel)
Field Officers: Mannoh W. Bateman (Major)
Duncan S. Cage (Lieutenant Colonel)
William C. Crow (Major, Lieutenant Colonel)
Winchester Hall (Colonel)
William W. Martin (Major)
Assignments: Coast Defenses, Department #1 (April-May 1862)
Department #1 (May 1862)
Jackson, Department #1 (May-June 1862)
Smith's Brigade, Department of Southern Mississippi and East Louisiana (June-July 1862)
Smith's Brigade, District of the Mississippi, Department #2 (July 1862)
2nd/3rd Sub-district, District of the Mississippi, Department #2 (July-October 1862)
Department of Mississippi and East Louisiana (October 1862)
2nd Military District, Department of Mississippi and East Louisiana (October-December 1862)

Thomas' Brigade, Lee's Provisional Division, 2nd Military District, Department of Mississippi and East Louisiana (December 1862)
Unattached, 2nd Military District, Department of Mississippi and East Louisiana (December 1862-January 1863)
Lee's Brigade, 2nd Military District, Department of Mississippi and East Louisiana (January 1863)
Lee's Brigade, Smith's Division, 2nd Military District, Department of Mississippi and East Louisiana (January-April 1863)
Lee's-Shoup's Brigade, Smith's Division, Department of Mississippi and East Louisiana (April-July 1863)
Thomas' Brigade, Polignac's Division, District of West Louisiana, Trans-Mississippi Department (August-September 1864)
1st (Thomas') Louisiana Brigade, 2nd (Polignac's-Thomas') Division, 1st Corps, Trans-Mississippi Department (September 1864-May 1865)
Battles: Vicksburg Bombardments (May 18-July 27, 1862)
Chickasaw Bayou (December 27-29, 1862)
vs. Steele's Bayou Expedition (March 14-27, 1863)
vs. Greenville Expedition (April 2-14, 1863)
Vicksburg Campaign (May-July 1863)
Vicksburg Siege (May-July 1863)
Further Reading: Hall, Winchester, *The Story of the 26th Louisiana Infantry in the Service of the Confederate States.*

182. LOUISIANA 27TH INFANTRY REGIMENT

Organization: Organized at Camp Moore in April 1862. Regiment surrendered at Vicksburg, Warren County, Mississippi on July 4, 1863. Paroled at Vicksburg, Warren County, Mississippi in July 1863. Declared exchanged in the fall of 1863. Those members of the regiment east of the Mississippi River was consolidated with similar portions of the 3rd, 17th, 21st (Smith's-Higgins'-Patton's), 22nd (Theard's-Herrick's), 26th, 29th and 31st Infantry Regiments and designated as the 22nd Consolidated Infantry Regiment at Enterprise, Mississippi on January 26, 1864. They became part of Company F, of that regiment. Balance of regiment reorganized at Alexandria in the summer of 1864. Surrendered by General E. K. Smith, commanding Trans-Mississippi Department, on May 26, 1865.
First Commander: Leon D. Marks (Colonel)
Field Officers: Jesse M. Cooper (Major)
Laurin L. McLaurin (Lieutenant Colonel)
Alexander S. Norwood (Major, Colonel)
George Tucker (Major)
Assignments: Coast Defenses, Department #1 (April-May 1862)

Department #1 (May 1862)
Defenses of Vicksburg, Department #1 (May-June 1862)
Smith's Brigade, Department of Southern Mississippi and East Louisiana (June-July 1862)
Smith's Brigade, District of the Mississippi, Department #2 (July 1862)
2nd/3rd Sub-district, District of the Mississippi, Department #2 (July-October 1862)
Department of Mississippi and East Louisiana (October 1862)
2nd Military District, Department of Mississippi and East Louisiana (October-December 1862)
Unattached, 2nd Military District, Department of Mississippi and East Louisiana (December 1862-January 1863)
Unattached, Smith's Division, 2nd Military District, Department of Mississippi and East Louisiana (January-February 1863)
Lee's Brigade, Smith's Division, 2nd Military District, Department of Mississippi and East Louisiana (March-April 1863)
Lee's-Shoup's Brigade, Smith's Division, Department of Mississippi and East Louisiana (April-July 1863)
Thomas' Brigade, Polignac's Division, District of West Louisiana, Trans-Mississippi Department (August 1863-September 1864)
Scott's Brigade, Adams' Cavalry Division, Department of Alabama, Mississippi, and East Louisiana [Companies A & D; mounted] (May-June 1864)
1st (Thomas') Louisiana Brigade, 2nd (Polignac's) Division, 1st Corps, Trans-Mississippi Department (September 1864-May 1865)
Battles: Vicksburg Bombardments (May 18-July 27, 1862)
vs. Greenville Expedition (April 2-14, 1863)
Vicksburg Campaign (May-July 1863)
Vicksburg Siege (May-July 1863)

183. LOUISIANA 28TH INFANTRY REGIMENT

Organization: Organized at Monroe ca. May 27, 1862. Surrendered by General E. K. Smith, commanding Trans-Mississippi Department, on May 26, 1865.
First Commander: Henry Gray (Colonel)
Field Officers: Isaac W. Melton (Lieutenant Colonel)
Thomas W. Pool (Major, Colonel)
William Walker (Lieutenant Colonel)
Assignments: Trans-Mississippi Department (May-August 1862)
District of West Louisiana, Trans-Mississippi Department (August-September 1862)
Mouton's Brigade, District of West Louisiana, Trans-Mississippi Department (October 1862-September 1863)

Mouton's Brigade, Sub-district of Southwestern Louisiana, District of West Louisiana, Trans-Mississippi Department (September-November 1863)
Mouton's-Grey's Brigade, Mouton's-Polignac's Division, District of West Louisiana, Trans-Mississippi Department (November 1863-September 1864)
1st (Thomas') Louisiana Brigade, 2nd (Polignac's) Division, 1st Corps, Trans-Mississippi Department (September 1864-May 1865)
Battles: Atchafalaya River *vs.* USS *Diana* [detachment] (March 28, 1863)
Fort Bisland (April 13-14, 1863)
Irish Bend (April 14, 1863)
Stirling's Plantation (September 29, 1863)
Red River Campaign (May 10-22, 1864)
Mansfield (April 8, 1864)
Pleasant Hill (April 9, 1864)
Yellow Bayou (May 18, 1864)

184. LOUISIANA 28TH (THOMAS') INFANTRY REGIMENT

See: LOUISIANA 29TH INFANTRY REGIMENT

185. LOUISIANA 29TH INFANTRY REGIMENT

Also Known As: Louisiana 28th (Thomas') Infantry Regiment
Organization: Organized on May 3, 1862. Regiment surrendered at Vicksburg, Warren County, Mississippi on July 4, 1863. Paroled at Vicksburg, Warren County, Mississippi in July 1863. Those members of the regiment east of the Mississippi River was consolidated with similar portions of the 3rd, 17th, 21st (Smith's-Higgins'-Patton's), 22nd (Theard's-Herrick's), 26th, 27th, and 31st Infantry Regiments and designated as the 22nd Consolidated Infantry Regiment at Enterprise, Mississippi on January 26, 1864. They became part of Company G, of that regiment. The balance of the regiment was reorganized at Alexandria in the summer of 1864. Surrendered by General E. K. Smith, commanding Trans-Mississippi Department, on May 26, 1865.
First Commander: Allen Thomas (Colonel)
Field Officers: Joseph O. Landry (Lieutenant Colonel, Colonel)
Charles M. Pegues (Major, Lieutenant Colonel)
Assignments: Department #1 (May 1862)
Defenses of Vicksburg, Department #1 (May-June 1862)
Smith's Brigade, Department of Southern Mississippi and East Louisiana (June-July 1862)
Smith's Brigade, District of the Mississippi, Department #2 (July 1862)
2nd/3rd Sub-district, District of the Mississippi, Department #2 (July-October 1862)
Department of Mississippi and East Louisiana (October 1862)

2nd Military District, Department of Mississippi and East Louisiana (October-December 1862)
Thomas' Brigade, Lee's Provisional Division, 2nd Military District, Department of Mississippi and East Louisiana (December 1862)
Unattached, 2nd Military District, Department of Mississippi and East Louisiana (December 1862-January 1863)
Lee's Brigade, 2nd Military District, Department of Mississippi and East Louisiana (January 1863)
Lee's Brigade, Smith's Division, 2nd Military District, Department of Mississippi and East Louisiana (January-April 1863)
Lee's-Shoup's Brigade, Smith's Division, Department of Mississippi and East Louisiana (April-July 1863)
Lee's-Shoup's Brigade, Smith's Division, Department of Mississippi and East Louisiana (April-July 1863)
Thomas' Brigade, Polignac's Division, District of West Louisiana, Trans-Mississippi Department (August-September 1864)
1st (Thomas') Louisiana Brigade, 2nd (Polignac's-Thomas') Division, 1st Corps, Trans-Mississippi Department (September 1864-May 1865)
Battles: Vicksburg Bombardments (May 18-July 27, 1862)
Chickasaw Bayou (December 27-29, 1862)
vs. Greenville Expedition (April 2-14 1863)
Vicksburg Campaign (May-July 1863)
Vicksburg Siege (May-July 1863)

186. LOUISIANA 30TH INFANTRY BATTALION

Organization: Organized by the reduction of the 30th Infantry Regiment to a battalion of seven companies on March 4, 1863. Detachment surrendered at Port Hudson, Louisiana on July 8, 1863. Paroled in July 1863. Field consolidation with the 4th and 13th Infantry Regiments from March 10 to May 4, 1865. Surrendered by Lieutenant General Richard Taylor, commanding the Department of Alabama, Mississippi, and East Louisiana, at Citronelle, Alabama on May 4, 1865.
First Commander: Thomas Shields (Lieutenant Colonel)
Field Officers: Charles J. Bell (Major)
Arthur Picolet (Major)
Assignments: Maxey's Brigade, 3rd Military District, Department of Mississippi and East Louisiana (March-May 1863)
Miles' Brigade, 3rd Military District, Department of Mississippi and East Louisiana [detachment] (May-July 1863)
Maxey's Brigade, Loring's Division, Department of the West [battalion] (May-June 1863)

Maxey's Brigade, French's Division, Department of the West [battalion] (June-July 1863)
Maxey's Brigade, French's Division, Department of Mississippi and East Louisiana [battalion] (July-August 1863)
Cantey's Brigade, Department of the Gulf (September-November 1863)
Quarles' Brigade, Breckinridge's Division, 2nd Corps, Army of Tennessee (November 1863-January 1864)
Quarles' Brigade, Department of the Gulf (February-April 1864)
Quarles' Brigade, District of the Gulf, Department of Alabama, Mississippi, and East Louisiana (April-May 1864)
Quarles' Brigade, Walthall's Division, Army of Mississippi (June 1864)
Gibson's Brigade, Stewart's-Clayton's Division, 2nd Corps, Army of Tennessee (June 1864-February 1865)
Gibson's Brigade, District of the Gulf, Department of Alabama, Mississippi, and East Louisiana (February-April 1865)
Gibson's Brigade, Department of Alabama, Mississippi, and East Louisiana (April-May 1865)
Battles: Vicksburg Campaign (May-July 1863)
Port Hudson Siege [detachment] (May-July 1863)
Jackson Siege (July 10-17, 1863)
Atlanta Campaign (May-September 1864)
New Hope Church (May 25-June 4, 1864)
Atlanta (July 22, 1864)
Ezra Church (July 28, 1864)
Atlanta Siege (July-September 1864)
Jonesboro (August 31-September 1, 1864)
Nashville (December 15-16, 1864)
Mobile (March 17-April 12, 1865)
Spanish Fort (March 27-April 8, 1865)

187. LOUISIANA 30TH INFANTRY REGIMENT

Nickname: Sumter Regiment
Organization: Organized in state service at New Orleans in December 1861. Mustered into state service at New Orleans on December 17, 1861. Transferred to Confederate service for 90 days on March 1, 1862. Part of the regiment surrendered at New Orleans on April 26, 1862. Reorganized with ten companies at Camp Moore on May 15, 1862. Reduced to a battalion of seven companies on March 4, 1863.
First Commander: Gustavus A. Breaux (Colonel)
Field Officers: Charles J. Bell (Major)
Thomas Shields (Lieutenant Colonel)

Assignments: Department #1 (December 1861-May 1862)
Port Hudson, Department #1 (April-June 1862)
Department of Southern Mississippi and East Louisiana (June-July 1862)
1st Sub-district, District of the Mississippi, Department #2 (July-October 1862)
Allen's Brigade, Ruggles' Division, Breckinridge's Command, District of the Mississippi, Department #2 [battalion] (August 1862)
Department of Mississippi and East Louisiana (October 1862)
3rd Military District, Department of Mississippi and East Louisiana (October-December 1862)
Maxey's Brigade, 3rd Military District, Department of Mississippi and East Louisiana (December 1862-March 1863)
Battles: New Orleans (April 18-25, 1862)
Baton Rouge [battalion] (August 5, 1862)

188. LOUISIANA 31ST INFANTRY REGIMENT

Organization: Organized by the increase of the 6th (Morrison's) Infantry Battalion to a regiment at Monroe on June 11, 1862. Catahoula Infantry Battalion merged into this regiment at Jackson, Mississippi in November 1862. Regiment surrendered at Vicksburg, Warren County, Mississippi on July 4, 1863. Paroled at Vicksburg, Warren County, Mississippi in July 1863. Those members remaining east of the Mississippi River were consolidated with similar portions of the 3rd, 17th, 21st (Smith's-Higgins'-Patton's), 22nd (Theard's-Herrick's), 26th, 27th, and 29th Infantry Regiments and designated as the 22nd Consolidated Infantry Regiment at Enterprise, Mississippi on January 26, 1864. They became part of company F of that regiment. Those members west of the Mississippi River reorganized at Minden, Louisiana in June 1864. Surrendered by General E. K. Smith, commanding Trans-Mississippi Department, on May 26, 1865.
First Commander: Charles H. Morrison (Colonel)
Field Officers: James W. Draughton (Major)
Sidney H. Griffin (Lieutenant Colonel)
Thomas C. Humble (Major)
Assignments: Department #1 (June-August 1862)
District of West Louisiana, Trans-Mississippi Department (August-November 1862)
Thomas' Brigade, Lee's Provisional Division, 2nd Military District, Department of Mississippi and East Louisiana (December 1862)
Unattached, 2nd Military District, Department of Mississippi and East Louisiana (December 1862-January 1863)
Lee's Brigade, Smith's Division, 2nd Military District, Department of Mississippi and East Louisiana (January-February 1863)

Baldwin's Brigade, Smith's Division, 2nd Military District, Department of Mississippi and East Louisiana (March-April 1863)
Baldwin's Brigade, Smith's Division, Department of Mississippi and East Louisiana (April-July 1863)
Thomas' Brigade, Polignac's Division, District of West Louisiana, Trans-Mississippi Department (June-September 1864)
1st (Thomas') Louisiana Brigade, 2nd (Polignac's-Thomas') Division, 1st Corps, Trans-Mississippi Department (September 1864-May 1865)
Battles: Chickasaw Bayou (December 27-29, 1862)
Vicksburg Campaign (May-July 1863)
Port Gibson (May 1, 1863)
Vicksburg Siege (May-July 1863)
Stirling's Plantation, Louisiana (September 29, 1863)

189. LOUISIANA 32ND INFANTRY REGIMENT

See: LOUISIANA MILES' LEGION, INFANTRY BATTALION

190. LOUISIANA 33RD INFANTRY REGIMENT

Organization: Organized by the consolidation of the Confederate (Louisiana) Guards Response and 10th Infantry Battalions near Donaldsonville ca. October 10, 1862. Broken up and the battalion organizations restored on November 22, 1862.
First Commander: Franklin H. Clack (Colonel)
Field Officers: Gabriel A. Fournet (Major)
Valsin A. Fournet (Lieutenant Colonel)
Assignments: District of West Louisiana, Trans-Mississippi Department (October 1862)
Mouton's Brigade, District of West Louisiana, Trans-Mississippi Department (October 1862-November 1863)
Battle: Georgia Landing, near Labadieville (October 27, 1862)

191. LOUISIANA BEAUREGARD INFANTRY REGIMENT, MILITIA

Organization: Called into Confederate service on March 1, 1862. Mustered out in May 1862. Again called briefly into service in May 1863.
First Commander: Frank A. Bartlett (Colonel)
Field Officers: George S. Lacey (Lieutenant Colonel)
George McKnight (Major)
Assignments: 2nd (Tracy's) Brigade, Louisiana State Troops, Department #1 (March-May 1862)
District of West Louisiana, Trans-Mississippi Department (May 1863)
Battles: New Orleans [not engaged] (April 18-25, 1862)

Caledonia and Pin Hook (May 10, 1863)

192. LOUISIANA CATAHOULA INFANTRY BATTALION

Organization: Organized with two companies in Mississippi on May 4, 1862. Merged into the 31st Infantry Regiment at Jackson, Mississippi in November 1862. This battalion does not appear in the *Official Records*.
First Commander: John Ker (Major [acting])
Field Officer: Rufus J. Bruce (Major [acting temporarily])
Assignments: Department #1 (May-June 1862)
Department of Southern Mississippi and East Louisiana (June-July 1862)
2nd Sub-district, District of the Mississippi, Department #2 (July 1862)
District of the Mississippi, Department #2 (July-October 1862)
Department of Mississippi and East Louisiana (October 1862)
Battle: Vicksburg Bombardments (May 18-July 27, 1862)

193. LOUISIANA CAZADORES ESPANOLES INFANTRY REGIMENT, MILITIA

Organization: Called into Confederate service ca. March 1, 1862. Mustered out in May 1862.
First Commander: Juan Miangolora (Major, Colonel)
Field Officers: Josi M. Auguera (Lieutenant Colonel)
Gaudenzi Marzoni (Major)
Neville Souli (Lieutenant Colonel)
Assignment: Department #1 (March-May 1862)
Battle: New Orleans [not engaged] (April 18-25, 1862)

194. LOUISIANA CHALMETTE INFANTRY REGIMENT, MILITIA

Organization: Called into Confederate service for 90 days ca. March 1, 1862. Mustered out in May 1862. Again called briefly into service in May 1863.
First Commander: Ignatius Szymanski (Colonel)
Field Officers: George W. Logan (Lieutenant Colonel)
Eugene Soniat (Major)
Assignments: Department #1 (March 1862)
Coast Defenses [Duncan's Command], Department #1 (March-April 1861)
Department #1 (April-May 1862)
District of West Louisiana, Trans-Mississippi Department (May 1863)
Battles: New Orleans (April 18-25, 1862)
Quarantine Battery (April 24, 1861)
Fort Beauregard (May 10-11, 1863)

195. LOUISIANA CHALMETTE CONSOLIDATED INFANTRY REGIMENT

Organization: Organized by the consolidation of the 13th and 16th Infantry Regiments in April 1865. Surrendered by Lieutenant General Richard Taylor, commanding the Department of Alabama, Mississippi, and East Louisiana, at Citronelle, Alabama on May 4, 1865.

Assignment: Gibson's Brigade, Department of Alabama, Mississippi, and East Louisiana (April-May 1865)

196. LOUISIANA CHASSEURS-À-PIED INFANTRY BATTALION

See: LOUISIANA 7TH INFANTRY BATTALION

197. LOUISIANA CHASSEURS-À-PIED INFANTRY REGIMENT, MILITIA

Organization: Called into Confederate service ca. March 1, 1862. Mustered out in May 1862.

First Commander: J. Simon Meilleur (Colonel)

Field Officers: C. A. Janvier (Lieutenant Colonel)

H. J. Rivet (Major)

Assignment: Department #1 (March-May 1862)

Battle: New Orleans [not engaged] (April 18-25, 1862)

198. LOUISIANA CLACK'S INFANTRY BATTALION

See: LOUISIANA CONFEDERATE GUARDS RESPONSE INFANTRY BATTALION

199. LOUISIANA CONFEDERATE GUARDS RESPONSE INFANTRY BATTALION

Also Known As: Louisiana 12th Infantry Battalion, Louisiana 16th Infantry Battalion

Organization: Organized with two companies at New Orleans on March 6, 1862. Field consolidation with the 1st Florida Infantry Battalion as the Florida and Confederate Guards Infantry Battalion from April 1862 to July 17, 1862. The battalion reorganized at New Iberia in August 1862. A third company joined the battalion on September 20, 1862. Consolidated with the 10th Infantry Battalion and designated as the 33rd Infantry Regiment ca. October 10, 1862. This regiment was broken up and the battalions reorganized on November 21, 1862. Companies D and E joined the battalion at Alexandria in the June 1864. However, Company D was a heavy artillery battery and continued to act as such independently. Company F was assigned to the battalion at Vermilionville in August 1864. Field consolidation with the 11th Infantry Battalion and Crescent Infantry Regiment from September 1864 to

October 1864. Permanently consolidated with the 11th Infantry Battalion and Crescent Infantry Regiment and designated as the Crescent Consolidated Infantry Regiment on November 3, 1863.

First Commander: Franklin H. Clack (Major, Lieutenant Colonel)

Assignments: Anderson's Brigade, Ruggles-Cheatham's Division, 2nd Corps, Army of the Mississippi, Department #2 (March-April 1862)

Moore's Brigade, Cheatham's-Ruggles' Division, 2nd Corps, Army of the Mississippi, Department #2 (April-May 1862)

Anderson's Brigade, 2nd Corps, Army of the Mississippi, Department #2 (June-July 1862)

Anderson's Brigade, Jones' Division, Army of the Mississippi, Department #2 (July-August 1862)

Mouton's Brigade, District of West Louisiana, Trans-Mississippi Department (November 1862-November 1863)

Battles: Shiloh (April 6-7, 1862)

Corinth Campaign (April-June 1862)

Farmington (May 9, 1862)

Fort Bisland (April 13-14, 1863)

Irish Bend (April 14, 1863)

Stirling's Plantation (September 29, 1863)

200. LOUISIANA CONFEDERATE GUARDS INFANTRY REGIMENT, MILITIA

Organization: Called into service ca. March 1, 1862. Mustered out in May 1862.

First Commander: John F. Girault (Colonel)

Field Officers: John I. Noble (Major)

Charles R. Railey (Lieutenant Colonel)

Assignment: Department #1 (March-May 1862)

Battle: New Orleans [not engaged] (April 18-25, 1862)

201. LOUISIANA CONTINENTAL INFANTRY REGIMENT, MILITIA

Organization: Called into service on March 1, 1862. Mustered out in May 1862.

First Commander: George Clark (Colonel)

Field Officers: George H. Hynson (Major)

Albert W. Merriam (Lieutenant Colonel)

Assignment: 2nd (Tracy's) Brigade, Louisiana State Troops, Department #1 (March-May 1862)

Battle: New Orleans [not engaged] (April 18-25, 1862)

202. LOUISIANA CRESCENT INFANTRY REGIMENT

Also Known As: Louisiana 24th Infantry Regiment

Organization: A militia unit. Organized for 90 days in Confederate service on March 6, 1862. Disbanded on June 3, 1862. Reorganized on November 17, 1862. Consolidated with the 11th and Confederate Guards Response Infantry Battalions and designated as the Crescent Consolidated Infantry Regiment at Simmesport on November 3, 1863.

First Commander: Marshal J. Smith (Colonel)

Field Officers: James H. Beard (Major, Lieutenant Colonel)

Abel W. Bosworth (Major, Colonel)

Myford McDougall (Major)

George P. McPheeters (Lieutenant Colonel, Colonel)

George Soule (Lieutenant Colonel)

Assignments: Department #1 (March 1862)

Pond's Brigade, Ruggles' Division, 2nd Corps, Army of the Mississippi, Department #2 (March-April 1862)

Ruggles' Brigade, Cheatham's-Ruggles' Division, 2nd Corps, Army of the Mississippi, Department #2 (April 1862-June 1863)

L. M. Walker's Brigade, 2nd Corps, Army of the Mississippi, Department #2 (June-July 1862)

L. M. Walker's Brigade, Jones' Division, Army of the Mississippi, Department #2 (July 1862)

Mouton's Brigade, District of West Louisiana, Trans-Mississippi Department (October 1862-November 1863)

Battles: Shiloh (April 6-7, 1862)

Corinth Campaign (April-June 1862)

Georgia Landing, near Labadieville (October 27, 1862)

Grand River [Companies F, G, and H] (February 16, 1863)

Fort Bisland (April 13-14, 1863)

203. LOUISIANA CRESCENT CONSOLIDATED INFANTRY REGIMENT

Also Known As: Louisiana 24th Infantry Regiment

Organization: Organized with 14 companies by the consolidation of the 11th and Confederate Guards Response Infantry Battalions and the Crescent Infantry Regiment at Simmesport on November 2, 1863. Surrendered by General E. K. Smith, commanding Trans-Mississippi Department, on May 26, 1865.

First Commander: James H. Beard (Colonel)

Field Officers: Abel W. Bosworth (Colonel)

Mercer Canfield (Major)

Franklin H. Clack (Lieutenant Colonel)

Arthur W. Hyatt (Lieutenant Colonel)
Hugh W. Montgomery (Major)
James J. Yarborough (Major)
Assignments: Mouton's-Gray's Brigade, Mouton's-Polignac's Division, District of West Louisiana, Trans-Mississippi Department (November 1863-September 1864)
2nd (Gray's) Louisiana Brigade, 2nd (Polignac's) Division, 1st Corps, Trans-Mississippi Department (September 1864-May 1865)
Battles: Red River Campaign (May 10-22, 1864)
Mansfield (April 8, 1864)
Pleasant Hill (April 9, 1864)
Yellow Bayou (May 18, 1864)
Atchafalaya River (June 8, 1864)

204. LOUISIANA DEFENDERS INFANTRY BATTALION

Organization: Organized with three companies at New Orleans in November 1861. Transferred to Confederate service on March 18, 1862. Apparently broken up on May 20, 1862. This battalion does not appear in the *Official Records.*
First Commander: Juan Miangolora (Major)
Assignment: Department #1 (November 1861-May 1862)

205. LOUISIANA DUPEIRE'S ZOUAVES INFANTRY BATTALION

See: LOUISIANA 2ND ZOUAVES INFANTRY BATTALION

206. LOUISIANA GOBER'S MOUNTED INFANTRY REGIMENT

Organization: Organized in June 1864. The six Louisiana companies of Powers' (Confederate) Cavalry Regiment were merged into this regiment in October 1864. Disbanded with the companies from Powers' Confederate Cavalry Regiment returning to their previous organization, the 18th Louisiana Cavalry Battalion and the balance of the regiment being assigned to Ogden's Cavalry Regiment in January 1865.
First Commander: Daniel C. Gober (Colonel)
Field Officers: Thomas Bynum (Major)
Haley M. Carter (Lieutenant Colonel)
James T. Coleman (Major)
Assignments: Scott's Brigade, W. Adams' Cavalry Division, Department of Alabama, Mississippi, and East Louisiana (June-August 1864)
Scott's Cavalry Brigade, District South of Homochitto, Department of Alabama, Mississippi, and East Louisiana (August-October 1864)

[Sub-]District of Southwest Mississippi and East Louisiana, District of Mississippi and East Louisiana, Department of Alabama, Mississippi, and East Louisiana (October-December 1864)
Scott's Cavalry Brigade, Northern Sub-district of Mississippi, District of Mississippi and East Louisiana, Department of Alabama, Mississippi, and East Louisiana (December 1864-January 1865)
Battles: Merritt's Plantation [skirmish] (May 18-19, 1863)
Doyal's Plantation [skirmish] (August 5, 1864)
Sara Bayou [skirmish] (October 4, 1864)
Thompson's Creek (October 5, 1864)
Woodville (October 5, 1864)
Expedition to Brookhaven (November 14-21, 1864)
Liberty [skirmish] (November 18, 1864)
Franklin (January 2, 1865)

207. LOUISIANA IRISH INFANTRY REGIMENT, MILITIA

Organization: Organized in Confederate service ca. March 1, 1862. Mustered out in May 1862.
First Commander: Patrick B. O'Brien (Colonel)
Field Officers: W. J. Castell (Lieutenant Colonel)
D. O. D. Sullivan (Major)
Assignment: Department #1 (March-May 1862)
Battle: New Orleans [not engaged] (April 18-25, 1862)

208. LOUISIANA JACKSON INFANTRY REGIMENT

See: LOUISIANA 21ST (KENNEDY'S) INFANTRY REGIMENT

209. LOUISIANA JEFF. DAVIS INFANTRY REGIMENT, MILITIA

Organization: Called into service on March 1, 1861. Mustered out in May 1861.
First Commander: Alexander Smith (Colonel)
Field Officers: John B. Cotton (Major)
William P. Freret (Lieutenant Colonel)
Assignment: 2nd (Tracy's) Brigade, Louisiana State Troops, Department #1 (March-May 1862)
Battle: New Orleans [not engaged] (April 18-25, 1862)

210. LOUISIANA JOHNSON'S SPECIAL INFANTRY BATTALION, MILITIA

Organization: Organized with five companies in Confederate service ca. March 1, 1862. Mustered out in May 1862.

First Commander: W. W. Johnson (Lieutenant Colonel)
Field Officer: W. H. Winn (Major)
Assignment: Department #1 (March-May 1862)
Battle: New Orleans [not engaged] (April 18-25, 1862)

211. LOUISIANA KEARY'S INFANTRY BATTALION

Organization: Organized with four companies completed on in June 1863. Disbanded on December 18, 1863.
First Commander: Patrick F. Keary (Major)
Assignment: Unattached, District of West Louisiana, Trans-Mississippi Department (June-December 1863)

212. LOUISIANA KING'S SPECIAL INFANTRY BATTALION, MILITIA

Organization: Organized with five companies in Confederate service ca. March 1, 1862. Mustered out in May 1862.
First Commander: John E. King (Lieutenant Colonel)
Assignment: Department #1 (March-May 1862)
Battle: New Orleans [not engaged] (April 18-25, 1862)

213. LOUISIANA LEEDS GUARDS INFANTRY REGIMENT, MILITIA

Organization: Organized in Confederate service ca. March 1, 1862. Mustered out in May 1862.
First Commander: Charles J. Leeds (Colonel)
Field Officers: A. G. Brice (Major)
E. Gunnell (Lieutenant Colonel)
Assignment: Department #1 (March-May 1862)
Battle: New Orleans [not engaged] (April 18-25, 1862)

214. LOUISIANA LEWIS INFANTRY BATTALION, MILITIA

Organization: Called into service on March 1, 1862. Mustered out in May 1862.
First Commander: William Tenbrink (Major)
Assignment: 2nd (Tracy's) Brigade, Louisiana State Troops, Department #1 (March-May 1862)
Battle: New Orleans [not engaged] (April 18-25, 1862)

215. LOUISIANA LOVELL INFANTRY BATTALION

See: LOUISIANA 6TH (REICHARD'S) INFANTRY BATTALION

216. LOUISIANA LOVELL INFANTRY REGIMENT

See: LOUISIANA 20TH INFANTRY REGIMENT

217. LOUISIANA MCCOWN INFANTRY REGIMENT

See: LOUISIANA 21ST (KENNEDY'S) INFANTRY REGIMENT

218. LOUISIANA MILES' LEGION INFANTRY BATTALION

Organization: Organized with eight companies at Camp Moore on May 16 or 17, 1862. Surrendered at Port Hudson, Louisiana on July 8, 1863. Paroled in July 1863. Declared exchanged prior to November 20, 1863. Those members east of the Mississippi River became part of Gober's Mounted Infantry Regiment in early 1864. Those members of the Legion west of the Mississippi River were reorganized as 15th Infantry Battalion Sharpshooters at Alexandria, Louisiana ca. July 1864. [NOTE: See also Louisiana Miles' Legion Cavalry Battalion; Louisiana Gibson's Artillery Battery; and Louisiana 2nd Siege Artillery Battery.]

First Commander: William R. Miles (Colonel)

Field Officers: Frank Brand (Lieutenant Colonel)
James T. Coleman (Major)
Robert C. Weatherly (Major)

Assignments: Port Hudson, Department #1 (May-June 1862)
Department of Southern Mississippi and East Louisiana (June-July 1862)
1st Sub-district, District of the Mississippi, Department #2 (July-October 1862)
Department of Mississippi and East Louisiana (October 1862)
3rd Military District, Department of Mississippi and East Louisiana (October 1862)
Maxey's Brigade, 3rd Military District, Department of Mississippi and East Louisiana (December 1862-February 1863)
Miles' Brigade, 3rd Military District, Department of Mississippi and East Louisiana (March 1863)
Buford's Brigade, 3rd Military District, Department of Mississippi and East Louisiana (March-April 1863)
Unattached, 3rd Military District, Department of Mississippi and East Louisiana (April-May 1863)
Miles' Brigade, 3rd Military District, Department of Mississippi and East Louisiana (May-July 1863)

Battles: Grand Gulf [detachment] (June 24, 1862)
vs. USS *Indianola* [detachment] (February 24, 1863)
Port Hudson Bombardment (March 14, 1863)
Grierson's Raid (April 17-May 2, 1863)
Plains Store (May 21, 1863)

Port Hudson Siege (May-July 1863)
Further Reading: Bergeron, Arthur, Jr. and Lawrence L. Hewitt, *Miles' Legion: A History and Roster.*

219. LOUISIANA ORLEANS FIRE INFANTRY REGIMENT

Organization: Organized in Confederate service ca. March 1, 1862. Mustered out in May 1862. This unit does not appear in the *Official Records*.
First Commander: S. P. Duncan (Colonel)
Field Officers: James D. Hill (Major)
M. M. Reynolds (Lieutenant Colonel)
Assignment: Department #1 (March-May 1862)
Battle: New Orleans [not engaged] (April 18-25, 1862)

220. LOUISIANA ORLEANS GUARD INFANTRY BATTALION

Organization: Organized from the Orleans Guard Infantry Regiment Militia for 90 days in Confederate service on March 6, 1862. Disbanded on June 6, 1862. NOTE: The Orleans Guard Artillery Battery was part of this corps.
First Commander: Leon Queyrouse (Major)
Assignment: Pond's Brigade, Ruggles' Division, 2nd Corps, Army of the Mississippi, Department #2 (March-April 1862)
Battles: Shiloh (April 6-7, 1862)
Corinth Campaign (April-June 1862)

221. LOUISIANA PELICAN CONSOLIDATED INFANTRY REGIMENT

Organization: Organized by the consolidation of the 4th Infantry Battalion, 19th, 20th, and 25th Infantry Regiments in April 1865. Surrendered by Lieutenant General Richard Taylor, commanding the Department of Alabama, Mississippi, and East Louisiana, at Citronelle, Alabama on May 4, 1865.
Assignment: Gibson's Brigade, Department of Alabama, Mississippi, and East Louisiana (April 1865-May 1865)

222. LOUISIANA PINKNEY INFANTRY BATTALION

See: LOUISIANA 8TH INFANTRY BATTALION AND LOUISIANA 8TH HEAVY ARTILLERY BATTALION

223. LOUISIANA RED RIVER INFANTRY BATTALION, SHARPSHOOTERS

See: LOUISIANA RED RIVER SCOUTS CAVALRY BATTALION

224. LOUISIANA ST. PAUL'S FOOT RIFLES INFANTRY BATTALION

See: LOUISIANA 7TH INFANTRY BATTALION

225. LOUISIANA STEWART'S INFANTRY LEGION

Organization: Organization attempted in early 1862. Failed to complete its organization. One cavalry and three infantry companies were designated as the 9th Infantry Battalion at Camp Moore on May 15, 1862.

First Commander: R. A. Stewart (Colonel)

Field Officer: Samuel Boyd (Lieutenant Colonel)

226. LOUISIANA SUMTER INFANTRY REGIMENT

See: LOUISIANA 30TH INFANTRY REGIMENT

227. LOUISIANA SUMTER INFANTRY REGIMENT, MILITIA

Organization: Called into Confederate service on March 1, 1862. Mustered out in May 1862.

First Commander: Gustavus P. Breaux (Colonel)

Field Officers: Charles Bell (Major)

Thomas Shields (Lieutenant Colonel)

Assignment: 2nd (Tracy's) Brigade, Louisiana State Troops, Department #1 (March-May 1862)

Battle: New Orleans [not engaged] (April 18-25, 1862)

228. LOUISIANA TERRE BONNE INFANTRY REGIMENT, MILITIA

Organization: Called into service on June 27, 1862. Mustered out in late 1862.

First Commander: John R. Bisland (Colonel)

Field Officer: William L. Shaffer (Lieutenant Colonel)

Assignment: Mouton's Brigade, District of West Louisiana, Trans-Mississippi Department (October 1862)

Battle: Georgia Landing, near Labadieville (October 27, 1862)

229. LOUISIANA WASHINGTON INFANTRY BATTALION

See: LOUISIANA 7TH INFANTRY BATTALION

230. LOUISIANA WEATHERLY'S INFANTRY BATTALION

See: LOUISIANA 15TH INFANTRY BATTALION, SHARPSHOOTERS

231. LOUISIANA YELLOW JACKET INFANTRY BATTALION

See: LOUISIANA 10TH INFANTRY BATTALION

BIBLIOGRAPHY

Amman, William. *Personnel of the Civil War.* 2 volumes. New York: Thomas Yoseloff, 1961. Provides valuable information on local unit designations, general officers' assignments and organizational data on geographical commands.

Bergeron, Arthur W., Jr. *Guide to Louisiana Confederate Military Units 1861–1865.* Baton Rouge: Louisiana State University Press, 1989. An extremely valuable recent source.

Boatner, Mark Mayo III. *The Civil War Dictionary.* New York: David McKay Company, 1959. Provides thumbnail sketches of leaders, battles, campaigns, events and units.

Bowman, John S. *The Civil War Almanac.* New York: Facts On File, 1982. Basically a chronology, it is valuable for its 130 biographical sketches, many of them military personalities.

Daniel, Larry J. *Cannoneers in Gray: The Field Artillery of the Army of Tennessee, 1861–1865.* University, Alabama. University of Alabama Press, 1984. An excellent study of the artillery in the western theater.

Evans, Clement A., ed. *Confederate Military History.* 13 volumes. Atlanta: Confederate Publishing Company, 1899. Each volume of this series primarily provides the histories of one or two states. Each state military account was written by a different participant in the war, and they vary greatly in quality. All accounts, however, include biographies of the generals from their state. The lack of a comprehensive index is the major drawback of this work. Volume X includes the Louisiana chapter by John Dimitry.

Freeman, Douglas Southall. *Lee's Lieutenants: A Study in Command.* 3 volumes. New York: Charles Scribner's Sons, 1941–1946. The premier narrative study of the organizational and command structure of the Army of Northern Virginia.

———. *R.E. Lee: A Biography.* 4 volumes. New York: Charles Scribner's Sons, 1934–1935. Also provides organizational information on the Army of Northern Virginia.

Johnson, Robert Underwood, and Buel, Clarence Clough, eds. *Battle and Leaders of the Civil War*. 4 volumes. New York: The Century Company, 1887. Reprinted 1956. Exceptionally valuable for its tables of organization for major engagements.

Krick, Robert K. *Lee's Colonels: A Biographical Register of the Field Officers of the Army of Northern Virginia*. 2nd edition. Dayton, Ohio: Press of Morningside Bookstore, 1984. Brief but very informative sketches of the 1,965 field-grade officers who at one time or another served with the Army of Northern Virginia but never achieved the the rank of brigadier general. The second edition also includes a listing by name and unit of those field-grade officers who never served with Lee.

Long, E.B. and Barbara. *The Civil War Day By Day: An Almanac 1861–1865*. Garden City, New York: Doubleday, 1971. An excellent chronology of the conflict, with much information on the organizational changes command assignments.

Lonn, Ella. *Foreigners in the Confederacy*. Chapel Hill: University of North Carolina, 1940. Accounts of the foreign-born contribution to the Confederacy.

National Archives, Record Group 109. Microfilm compilation of the service records of every known Confederate soldier, organized by unit. The caption cards and record-of-events cards at the beginning of each unit provide much valuable information on the units' organizational history.

Scharf, J. Thomas. *History of the Confederate States Navy: From Its Organization to the Surrender of Its Last Vessels*. Albany: Joseph McDonough, 1887. A rather disjointed narrative that provides some insight into operations along the Southern coast and on the inland waterways. Unfortunately, it lacks an adequate index.

Sifakis, Stewart. *Who Was Who in the Civil War*. New York: Facts On File, 1988.

———. *Who Was Who in the Confederacy*. New York: Facts On File, 1989. Together both works include biographies of over 1,000 participants who served the South during the Civil War. The military entries include much information on regiments and higher commands.

U.S. Navy Department. *Official Records of the Union and Confederate Navies in the War of the Rebellion*. 31 volumes. Washington: Government Printing Office, 1894–1927. Provides much valuable information on the coastal and riverine operations of the Civil War.

U.S. War Department. *The War of the Rebellion: A Compilation of the Official Records of the Union and Confederate Armies*. 70 volumes in 128 books divided into four series, plus atlas. Washington: Government Printing Office, 1881–1901. While difficult to use, this set provides a gold mine of information. Organized by campaigns in specified geographic regions, the volumes are divided into postaction reports and correspondence. The information contained in the hundreds of organizational tables proved invaluable for my purposes.

Wakelyn, Jon L. *Biographical Dictionary of the Confederacy*. Westport, Conn.: Greenwood Press, 1977. Short biographies of 651 leaders of the Confederacy. However, the selection criteria among the military leaders is somewhat haphazard.

Warner Ezra J. *Generals in Gray: Lives of the Confederate Commanders*. Baton Rouge: Louisiana State University Press, 1959. Sketches of the 425 Southern generals. Good coverage of pre- and postwar careers. The wartime portion of the entries leaves something to be desired.

Wise, Jennings Cropper. *The Long Arm of Lee: The History of the Artillery of the Army of Northern Virginia*. Lynchburg, Virginia: J.P. Bell Co., 1915. Reprinted 1959. An excellent study of Lee's artillery, providing valuable information on batteries and their commanders and organizational assignments.

Wright, Marcus J. *General Officers of the Confederate Army*. New York: Neale Publishing Co., 1911. Long the definitive work on the Confederate command structure, it was superseded by Ezra J. Warner's work.

PERIODICALS

Civil War Times Illustrated, its predecessor *Civil War Times*, *American History Illustrated* and *Civil War History*. In addition, the *Southern Historical Society Papers* (47 vols., 1876–1930) are a gold mine of information on Confederate units and leaders.

LOUISIANA BATTLE INDEX

References are to record numbers, not page numbers.

LOUISIANA NAME INDEX

References are to record numbers, not page numbers.